atrium

Werner Blaser

atrium

Lichthöfe seit fünf Jahrtausenden   Five thousand years of open courtyards

Mit einer Einführung   With an introduction
von Johannes Spalt   by Johannes Spalt

Wepf & Co. AG Verlag

Text, Fotografien und Gestaltung:
Werner Blaser
Einführung:
Johannes Spalt
Englische Übersetzung:
D.Q. Stephenson
Photolithos:
Steiner & Co. AG, Basel
Satz und Druck:
Werner Druck AG, Basel
Buchbinderei:
Grollimund AG, Reinach/BL
Verlag:
Wepf & Co. AG, Basel, New York

Text, photographs and lay-out:
Werner Blaser
Introduction:
Johannes Spalt
English translation:
D.Q. Stephenson
Photolithos:
Steiner & Co. AG, Basel
Composition and printing:
Werner Druck AG, Basel
Binding:
Grollimund AG, Reinach/BL
Publishers:
Wepf & Co. AG, Basel, New York

CIP-Kurztitelaufnahme der Deutschen
Bibliothek
Blaser, Werner
Atrium: Lichthöfe seit 5 Jahrtsd.
= Atrium / Werner Blaser.
Mit e. Einf. von Johannes Spalt.
(Engl. Übers.: D.Q. Stephenson.)
Basel, New York: Wepf, 1985.

Library of Congress
Cataloging-in-Publication Data
Blaser, Werner, 1924–
Atrium: Lichthöfe seit fünf Jahrtausenden
= five thousand years of open courtyards.
English and German. Bibliography: p.
Includes index. 1. Courtyard houses.
2. Courtyards. 3. Atriums. 4. Atrium
buildings. I. Title.
NA7523.B5413 1985 720 85–12365

Inhalt

Contents

Die Geschichte des Hofhauses von
Johannes Spalt

The history of the courtyard house
by Johannes Spalt

Gehöft aus der Hallstattzeit, Rekonstruktion
Farmstead of the Hallstatt period, reconstruction

Aus dem Lied des Shi-King, 825 v. Chr.

‹Glatt strecken sich des Hofes Breiten,
Hoch ragen Pfeiler ihm zur Seiten,
Mild kann hinein die Helle gleiten,
Wo sich die stillen Räume weiten
Und Ruhm dem hohen Herrn bereiten!›

Die Philosophie des Hofraumes

Der Mensch braucht inmitten des Universums einen Raum des Friedens, der Geborgenheit, als Teil der grösseren, feindlichen, unbestimmten Aussenwelt, einen Raum, der trotzdem teilhat an Tag und Nacht, an Sonne und Mond, an Hitze, Kälte und Regen. Dieser Raum, der dem Tages- und Jahresablauf, also den das Dasein bestimmenden Regeln unterworfen ist, ist der ‹Hofraum›. Er ist einer der ältesten Raumformen und symbolisiert noch Empfindungen aus dem Höhlendasein des Menschen. Er gilt auch als Symbol der Weiblichkeit in Haus und Hof oder als Raumsymbol der Innerlichkeit. Dieser Hofraum gibt durch seine Abgeschlossenheit den Bewohnern die Illusion eines eingebildeten Herrschaftsbereiches, eben einer künstlichen Intimität. Der Mensch braucht Mauern, Zäune und Einfriedungen für das Vorstellungsbild eines ungefährdeten Daseins; daher erscheint uns die Beziehung zwischen

From the song of Shi-King, 825 BC

Evenly stretches the courtyard wide,
High stand the pillars on each side,
Softly therein the sunbeams glide,
Where the quiet rooms inside
Lie in peace, their great lord's pride.

The philosophy of the courtyard

Set in the midst of the universe, man needs a place of peace, seclusion, as part of the greater, hostile, amorphous world outside, a space which, all the same, receives its share of day and night, sun and moon, heat and cold and rain. This space, which is subservient to the passage of the days and years and to the rules that order existence, is the 'courtyard'. It is so old that sensations inherited from man's cave-dwelling days have been symbolized in it. It symbolizes femininity in the house and home; it is a spatial symbol of inwardness. Seclusion, the courtyard's artificially created seclusion, makes those who dwell there the inhabitants of an imaginary kingdom. To nurture this image of unimperilled existence, man needs walls, fences, enclosures, and therefore the relationship between imagined space and its inhabitants seems to be of fundamental importance. Whether other factors, functional

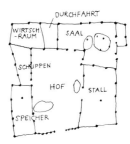

Hallstattzeitliches Gehöft in Neuhansel im Westerwald
Hallstattan farmstead at Neuhansel in the Westerwald

7

vorgestelltem Raum und seinen Bewohnern als wesentlich. Ob nun in späterer Zeit andere Ursachen dazu führten, die einmal gefundene Form durch funktionelle Notwendigkeit andersartig in Zusammenhang zu bringen, ist nicht erforscht, bleibt doch der Hof über die ganze lange Entwicklung die Mitte des Hauses, der zentrale, offene Platz im Gegensatz zu den geschlossenen Räumen.

Unter ‹Hof› versteht man meistens einen von Mauern umschlossenen Teil des Hauses oder wenigstens einen teilweise offenen Raum, der in der Menschheitsgeschichte eine wichtige Rolle spielt.

Die Form des Raumes im Grundriss muss nicht bestimmt sein, ob sie nun rund, quadratisch, rechteckig oder beliebig gekrümmt ist. Auch über die Grösse sagt das Wort nichts aus; der Ausdehnung sind jedoch Grenzen gesetzt, da eine gewisse Beziehung der Hofeinfassungswände existieren muss. Aus der Schrumpfung und dem immer Höherwerden der Wohnbauten hat sich der verpönte Lichthof als notwendig ergeben – der manchmal in den Spekulationsbauten nur zu einem Abluftschlauch wurde. Aus der Vielfalt der Bezeichnungen ist die Entwicklung und der Tätigkeitsbezug im Hof erkennbar. Ein Gartenhof sagt, dass eine gewisse Bepflanzung – wenigstens z.B. ein Baum – diesen Hof zum Garten stempelt. Andere Hofarten sind z.B.: Bau- und Werkhof, Klosterhof, Freihof, Schlosshof, Schulhof, Kaufhof, Wirtschaftshof und Friedhof. Dies sind feste Begriffe, die einen von Strassen und Plätzen sich unterscheidenden Bereich meinen.

Bei landwirtschaftlichen Gebäuden ist der Hof derjenige Wirtschaftsraum, der von Wohn- und Wirtschaftsräumen umschlossen wird. Noch immer sagen wir zu landwirtschaftlichen Gebäuden oder diesen mit dem umgebenden Grund ‹Hof›. Die Art des Gebäudes, das diesen Hof umschliesst, wird zum Beispiel in Oberösterreich mit Dreiseithof,

necessities, forced this form, once found, into other relationships, has never been investigated, but, all through long centuries of development, the court has remained the centre of the house, the open area in the middle as opposed to the closed rooms.

'Courtyard' usually suggests a part of the house shut in by walls, or at least a partly open room, and throughout history, it has played an important role. The courtyard plan need not be fixed; it can be round, square, rectangular or as curved in outline as desired. Nor has the word implications about size, but a certain relationship of the enclosing walls sets limits to its extent. As residential buildings have shrunk and grown ever higher, the despised air well has proved a necessity, dwindling sometimes in speculative buildings to a mere air shaft. The development and uses of the word courtyard are reflected in various prefixes it has acquired. A garden courtyard intimates planting – at least a tree – to mark it as a garden. And then there are other types which, while not necessarily containing the word 'courtyard', nevertheless refer to well-defined concepts meaning an area distinct from streets and squares: builder's yards, cloister garths, baileys, wards, school yards, inn yards and churchyards.

In the case of farm buildings the yard is the utility area adjoining the farmhouse and service-related facilities. Depending on the type of enclosing building, this yard is called, for example in Upper Austria, a 'Dreiseithof', a 'Vierseithof' or, in its purest formal expression, a 'Vierkanthof'. The cloister garth is an essential element in the development of the courtyard, for the earliest monastic buildings down to the great Baroque abbey contain many garths of interesting design.

Needless to say, orientation is of great importance in courts and not only because of exposure to the sun: indeed, even in ancient Egypt, the layout created links with the cosmos.

Wohnhaus in der 348 v. Chr. zerstörten Stadt Olynthos bei Saloniki. Es hat die Urform des Balkanhauses mit dem dreiseitig von Holzgalerien umgebenen Hof.
Dwelling house in the town of Olynthos (near Saloniki), which was destroyed in 348 B.C. It has the prototypal form of the Balkan house with the courtyard surrounded on three sides by wooden galleries.

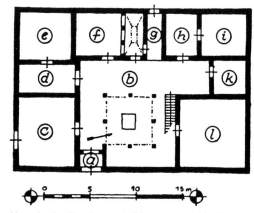

Haus in der Provinzstadt Olynthos auf Chalkidike, 600 v. Chr.
House on the Chalcidice of the provincial town of Olynthos, 600 B.C.

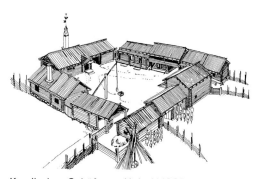

Karelisches Gehöft aus Holz, UdSSR
Karelian farmstead, timber-built, in the USSR

Vierseithof oder in reinster Formausprägung mit ‹Vierkanthof› bezeichnet. Der ‹Klosterhof› stellt einen wesentlichen Teil der Hofentwicklung dar, zeigen doch die frühesten Anlagen bis zu den grossen barocken Klöstern vielfältige und interessant gestaltete Höfe. Natürlich spielt bei den Höfen die Orientierung eine wichtige Rolle, nicht nur von der Besonnung ausgehend, vielmehr wurden schon im alten Ägypten kosmische Bezüge hergestellt. Historisch gesehen wurden im Hof viele Tätigkeiten ausgeübt, da er erst der Ort des Feuers war, doch hat man dort auch geschlafen – wie auch heute noch z.B. in maurischen und irakischen Häusern, in nischenartigen Rücksprüngen, die überdeckt waren; sie sind oft zweigeschossig und gegen den Hof offen. Die Bauweise, in der die den Hof umgebenden Räume von diesem Licht bekommen oder aufgeschlossen werden, unterscheidet sich von solchen Gebäuden, bei denen der Hof nur teilweise oder gar keine Fenster oder Türen zu den umliegenden Räumen hat. Ebenso bringt Ein- oder Mehrgeschossigkeit der Häuser und des Hofes andere Aufschliessungs- und Raumkomponenten mit sich. Eine weitere Unterscheidung wird durch geschlossene oder getrennte Baukörper getroffen, wie wir am chinesischen Pavillonhaus ersehen können. Die Beziehung zwischen Bewohnern und ihrem vorgestellten Raum ist von grosser Bedeutung. Der Hof als Raumsymbol der Innerlichkeit ist mit einer offenen Raumschachtel vergleichbar, einem ‹Schrank im Schrank›, in dem er einen Teil des unendlich grossen Raumes darstellt, auch durch seine Abgeschlossenheit. Auf ihn trifft der Mythos der Hohlform zu, eine ‹Insel der Glückseligen› zu sein. Dieser Mythos des Hauses und seines Hofes hat Nähe zum Archetypus der Mutter, die ein Symbol der Weiblichkeit ist. Diese Geschichte des Hofhauses ist eigentlich nur ein Vorbericht und kann nicht in Anspruch nehmen, eine im

Historically, the courtyard was the scene of many activities, for it was originally the place where the fire was kept burning, but it was also used for sleeping – just as is the custom today in Moorish and Iraqi houses – in covered alcoves set back in the wall; these are often two-storeyed and open on the courtyard side. The structural form in which the rooms surrounding the court obtain their light or access from it is different from that of buildings where the courtyard has few or no windows and doors to the surrounding rooms. Even so, the presence of one or more storeys in the houses and courts involves different modes of access and spatial components.
A further distinction is made by the presence of closed or separate buildings, as can be seen in the Chinese pavilion house.
The relationship between inhabitants and their imagined space is of great importance. As a spatial symbol of inwardness the courtyard is comparable to an open nest of spaces, one within another, where it is the surrogate of infinite space, an impression enhanced by its isolation. It embodies something of the myth of the hollow form, or being an 'Island of the Blessed'. This myth of the house and its courtyard approximates to the archetype of the mother, who is a symbol of femininity.
This history is actually only a preliminary account and cannot claim to be a true history of the courtyard house in the full sense, being more a sporadic and successive compilation from different periods and regions of the world. Thus an aspect neglected in previous publications will be presented. Examples of farm courtyards and courts in urban structures from the Biedermeier period in Vienna have been added. These represent a development of the single-storey Burgenland house; the examples shown also include multistorey types. The history of the courtyard house is only one part of the history of human dwellings. No work has ever been done

Maurischer Hof im Palast des Gouverneurs in Tanger, 17. Jh.
Moorish courtyard in the governor's palace at Tangiers, 17th cent.

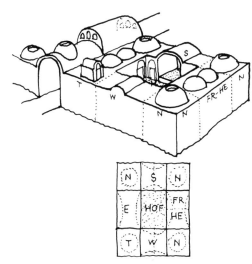

Yazt, typisches Wohnhaus mit gedeckter Gasse und Wohnhausschema
Yazt, typical dwelling house with covered street and residential layout

historischen Sinn wirkliche Geschichte des Hofhauses zu sein, sondern ist vielmehr eine sporadische und sukzessive Zusammenstellung aus verschiedenen Zeiten und Gegenden der Welt. Damit wird ein Bereich dargestellt, der bisher in ähnlichen Veröffentlichungen nicht behandelt wurde. Es wurden Hof-Beispiele aus dem bäuerlichen Bereich und städtische Objekte aus der Wiener Biedermeierzeit dazugewählt, die auf der einen Seite eine Weiterentwicklung des ebenerdigen Burgenlandhauses darstellen, andererseits werden auch mehrgeschossige Typen gezeigt.

Die Geschichte des Hofhauses ist nur ein Teil der Geschichte der Behausungen der Menschen. Diese Völker und Kontinente betreffende, spezifische Geschichte des Hauses wurde nie erarbeitet und zusammengestellt. Sie müsste in enzyklopädischer Form nicht nur die Formen in ihrer Entwicklung zeigen, sondern gleichfalls die gesellschaftlichen, sozialen und völkischen Charakteristika und ihre Auswirkungen, wie technische, formale und vom Material und Werkzeug her bedingte Prämissen. Natürlich spielten Klima, Licht, Vegetation und Topographie neben vielen anderen Voraussetzungen und Einwirkungen eine grosse Rolle. Die durch Verteidigung und Schutz bedingten baulichen kriegstechnischen Erfordernisse waren von einiger Bedeutung. Diese sicher aufregende Zusammenfassung mit typischen Beispielen käme einer Menschheitsgeschichte gleich, ist doch die ‹Behausung› (kommt von Hausen, Haus) das zweite, manchmal das alleinige Kleid des Menschen, sein grösseres oder kleineres Abbild seiner Aktionen, Wege und Tätigkeiten. Es ist anzunehmen, dass diese grosse, umfassende Hausgeschichte in uns eine andere Sicht auslösen würde als unser derzeitiges sporadisches, auf das Detail und auf begrenzte Orte hinorientiertes Wissen über Traditionen und Ursachen (‹Kleine Weltgeschichte des städtischen Wohnhauses›, Ludolf Veltheim-Lottum).

to compile a specific history of the house covering peoples and continents. It would have to be encyclopaedic in scale since it would show not only formal developments but also the social and ethnic characteristics and their effects as well as the technical and formal conditions imposed by working materials and tools. Needless to say, climate, light, vegetation and topography play an important role along with other background conditions and influences. The structural requirements needed for defence and protection were also of some importance. Such a compilation, illustrated with typical examples, would make fascinating reading and be equivalent to a history of humanity, for housing is the second, and sometimes even the only, clothing of man – an image, great or small, of his actions, his comings and goings, and his enterprises. This great and comprehensive history may well evoke in us a vision different from our present fragmentary and locally restricted knowledge of traditions, causes and influences affecting our activities and buildings ('Kleine Weltgeschichte des städtischen Wohnhauses', Ludolf Veltheim-Lottum).

The courtyard house, sometimes called the atrium house or garden-court house (although there are differences), is an early specialized form which usually relates to particular regions. However, it evolved all over the world and during every century, and sometimes, indeed, having become established, disappeared again.

Originally the word 'atrium' meant 'black' (focus), because it was there that the hearth was located and the ceiling of the room was darkened by the escaping smoke. In the beginning there was no opening in the roof of this hearth room and the smoke made its way out via the roof. Only after a lengthy development did this room, which served several functions, acquire an opening in its roof which, particularly after the hearth had been removed to another room of its own (kitchen),

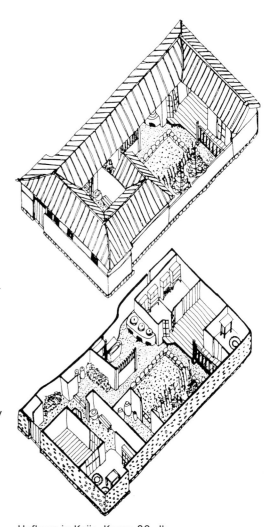

Hofhaus in Kajio, Korea, 20. Jh.
Courtyard house at Kajio, Korea, 20th cent.

Das Hofhaus, manchmal als Atriumhaus oder als Gartenhofhaus bezeichnet (trotzdem hier Unterschiede bestehen), ist eine frühe Sonderform, die sich meist auf bestimmte Gegenden bezieht, jedoch in allen Jahrhunderten und weltweit entwickelt wurde – ja, manchmal wieder verschwand.

In seiner ursprünglichen Form bezeichnet das Wort ‹Atrium› den Raum, in dem sich der Herd (focus) des Hauses befand; dieser Raum war durch den abziehenden Rauch an der Decke geschwärzt, da keine Öffnung vorhanden war, und der Rauch durch das Dach abzog. Erst in einer längeren Entwicklung bekam dieser Raum, der mehrere Funktionen erfüllte, eine Öffnung im Dach, die sich besonders nach Verlegung des Herdes zu einem eigenen Raum (Küche) vergrösserte und zum bekannten Begriff des Atriums sich ausbildete. Schon früh war es damit der Mittelpunkt des häuslichen Lebens, besonders durch die es umgebenden Räume, die teils offen durch Türen mit diesem zusammenhingen und das Licht von der Öffnung im Dach des Atriums erhielten. Ursprünglich nahm dieser Raum neben dem Herd das Ehebett, die Familiengötter (Laren und Penaten) und die Webstühle (Telar) auf. Mit der Steigerung der Ansprüche an das städtische Wohnhaus verwandelte sich das Atrium in einen Empfangssaal mit Wasserbecken, Brunnen und Rasenplätzen.

Die feudalen Häuser in Pompeji und Herculanum zeigen nach dem Atrium einen weiteren grösseren, von Säulen umgebenen Hof, das ‹Peristylium›, das durch die Fauces mit dem Atrium verbunden ist. Ebenso in viel späterer Zeit hat sich dieser mit Säulen umgebene Hof als ‹Kreuzgang› im Kloster erhalten, jedoch war dann der Kirchenkomplex der dominierende Teil.

Vitruvius unterscheidet das Atrium nach 5 Gruppen: das Tusculanum, das Tetrastylum, das korinthische Atrium, das Atrium dipluvium und das Schildkrötenatrium, das Testudinatum und gibt,

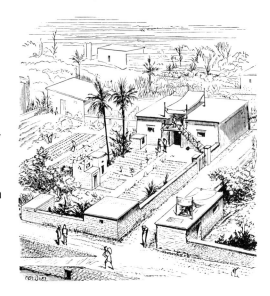

grew in size and developed into the atrium as we know it. It was not long before it had become the centre of domestic life, particularly because of the surrounding rooms, which sometimes formed a continuum with it through open doors and received their light from the opening in the atrium roof. Originally, besides the hearth, this room also contained the marriage bed, the family gods (lares and penates) and the looms (tela). As the urban house came to play a socially more exalted role, the atrium was converted into a reception room with a pool, fountain and lawn. In the feudal houses of Pompeii and Herculaneum there was, following on the atrium, another, larger courtyard surrounded by pillars called the 'peristylium', connected to the atrium by the fauces. In much later times this pillared courtyard became the cloister of the monastery, but by then the church complex had itself become the dominant part.

Vitruvius divided the atrium into five categories: the tusculanum, the tetrastylum, the corinthian atrium, the atrium dipluvium and the testudinatum or tortoise atrium and, with the square as a basis, gives 5:3 and 2:3 as the ratio; the peristyle should lie crosswise and be one third longer than wide. The great advantage of these atrium houses was that the principle could be retained even when more rooms were added, and further courtyards could be adjoined behind, like Chinese courtyard houses.

The age of the courtyard type of house goes far back into human history. The earliest known to us, dating from 3000 BC, were built in India and China. The courtyard houses at Knossos on Crete date from the years c. 2000 BC.

The climate was a factor of some importance in determining the spread of the courtyard house in particularly clement regions. But some of these houses have existed in harsh climates since the earli-

Hofhäuser in Ägypten, Rekonstruktionen
Courtyard houses in Egypt, reconstructions

ausgehend vom Quadrat, 5:3 und 2:3 als Verhältnis an, das Peristyl soll quer liegen und ein Drittel länger als breit sein. Diese Atriumhäuser hatten den grossen Vorteil, dass man das Prinzip auch bei Vermehrung der Räume beibehalten konnte und sich nach hinten weitere Höfe anschliessen konnten, ähnlich den chinesischen Hofhäusern.

Das Alter des Hofhaustyps reicht weit in die Menscheitsgeschichte zurück; die frühesten uns bekannten sind in Indien und China aus der Zeit um 3000 vor Christi. Die Hofhäuser in Knossos auf Kreta stammen aus der Zeit um ca. 2000 vor Christi.

Das Klima hatte eine gewisse Bedeutung bei der Verbreitung des Hofhauses in besonders begünstigten Gegenden. Wir kennen jedoch ebenso solche seit frühester Zeit in rauhem Klima. Grundsätzlich war das Hofhaus vorerst ein Stadthaus in der chinesischen, griechischen und römischen Kultur. Aus dieser Entwicklungsgeschichte würde uns eine andere Sicht als die gegenwärtige von unserer Baukultur vermittelt und die grosse Arroganz heutiger Tendenzen korrigiert. Es ist bekannt, dass die Entdeckung neuer Länder und ihrer Bewohner, aber auch Ausgrabungen vergangener Baukulturen grossen Einfluss auf unser westliches Bauen genommen haben (Pompeji, Ägypten u.a.). Ja, man könnte in manchen Fällen von Kopien sprechen; bekannt sind uns aus der Zeit des Historismus die pompejianische Wandmalerei und viele Details aus China im Barockstil. Als Beispiel solcher Beeinflussung aus neuerer Zeit wären das alte Schweizerhaus und später das englische Landhaus zu nennen. Vielleicht lernen wir aus der Geschichte des Hausbaues und seiner räumlichen Komposition, die immer in Zusammenhang mit unseren Lebensgewohnheiten steht und ein körperliches Abbild darstellt. Dieses zeichnet sich in Wegen und Plätzen auch innerhalb des Hauses

est days. Basically the courtyard house was a town house in the civilizations of China, Greece and Rome.

This historical review alters the perspective in which we look at things from the angle of our own architecture and corrects the arrogance of modern tendencies. Western architecture has been greatly influenced by the discovery of new countries and peoples and also by the excavations of past civilizations (Egypt, Pompeii, etc.). Indeed, it would be no exaggeration in some cases to speak of copies – witness Pompeian murals in historicism and many details from China embodied in the Baroque style. Similar influences have been exerted in more recent times by the old Swiss house and later by the English country house. Perhaps there is a lesson for us to learn from the history of house construction and its spatial composition, which is invariably moulded by our living habits and is an image made in our likeness. This is also reflected in the routes and places inside the house and is, in a way, the 'hollow form of our domestic existence'. It is hardly surprising, then, that there should have been an element of mysticism in house construction. Building a house is like a birth: one wants to propitiate the good spirits and exorcise the evil ones. Ever since the distant past when man emerged from his caves and primitive dwellings, social, medical and health factors have been important. Within the complex of the house, the atrium offered air, light and seclusion, and indeed peace. That is why the atrium became an open space that also served other purposes.

About 2000 BC in Ur they were building two-storey houses on an almost square plan with the rooms arranged round a courtyard. The building material was fired brick, the rainwater falling in the courtyard was led off through pipes. Entrance hall, kitchen, liwan and washroom were accommodated on the ground floor. The private rooms were upstairs.

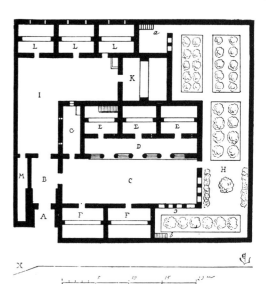

Haus in Pompeji, 1. Jahrhundert v. Chr.
House at Pompeii, 1st cent. B.C.

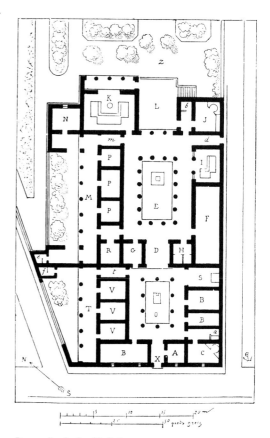

Pompejianische Hofhäuser
Pompeian courtyard houses

ab, ist gewissermassen die ‹Hohlform unserer häuslichen Existenz›. Es ist daher naheliegend, dass mit dem Hausbau immer auch Mystisches verbunden ist. Das Errichten eines Hauses gleicht einer Geburt, man will die guten Geister beschwören und die schlechten abhalten. Soziale und medizinische oder gesundheitliche Überlegungen spielen seit frühester Zeit, da der Mensch die Höhle und die Primitivbehausungen verlassen hat, eine grosse Rolle. Das Atrium bot innerhalb des Hauskomplexes Luft, Licht und Geborgenheit, ja Frieden. Daher wurde das Atrium auch zum anderen Zwecken dienenden Freiraum.

In der Zeit um 2000 vor Christi wurden in Ur 2geschossige Einfamilienhäuser mit fast quadratischem Grundriss, bei denen die Zimmer um einen Hof angeordnet sind, gebaut. Das Baumaterial waren gebrannte Ziegel; das Regenwasser des Hofes wurde mit Rohren abgeleitet. Das Erdgeschoss nahm Eingangshalle, Küche, Liwan und Waschraum auf. Das Obergeschoss war den Privaträumen vorbehalten.

Das griechische Megaronhaus mit einem Hof, der nur auf einer Seite Säulen aufwies, wurde direkt von der Strasse betreten; die Beispiele aus Delos und Priene zeigen in ihrer Rekonstruktion diesen Typ. Dieser Megarontyp wurde durch das asiatische Hofhaus verdrängt, indem man Obergeschosse aufgestockt hat. Den Höhepunkt der Hausentwicklung erkennen wir in der Blütezeit der griechischen Kultur im 4. und 5. Jahrhundert vor Christi. Das ‹Peristylhaus› bildet daher auch die Urform des orientalischen Hofhauses, es hat sich zeitlich verfeinert. Um einen Innenhof gab es in den vornehmen Häusern Empfangs- und Speisezimmer, aber auch Schlafräume, Wirtschaftsräume und im hinteren Abschnitt des Hauses Zimmer für Frauen. Gelegentlich hatte der Hof eine Galerie.

Die etruskische und griechische Kultur hatten entscheidenden Einfluss auf das

The Greek megaron house with a courtyard pillared on only one side was entered directly from the street; the reconstructed examples in Delos and Priene are of this type. This megaron house was replaced by the Asiatic courtyard house to which upper storeys were added. House development reached its apogee during the heyday of Greek civilization in the 4th and 5th centuries BC. The 'peristyle house' was therefore the original form of the oriental courtyard house and had grown more sophisticated with time. In the better class of house there were reception and dining rooms round the central court, but there were also bedrooms and utility rooms and, in the rear part of the house, rooms for the women. Sometimes the courtyard had a gallery. The Etruscan and Greek civilizations had a marked influence on the Roman house, and we may suppose that it was from the Etruscan house that the Roman atrium house developed as an all-in-one house with its living quarters and utility rooms under one roof. These houses, which were built side by side along the street, were single-storey structures and had no windows. The hearth with its smoke outlet was at the centre of the building, where there was no roof (atrium). This house received its light through the roof opening and from the house entrance. The 'atrium' was, as it were, the hall with the open roof, which ultimately assumed the form of a courtyard. Inside this courtyard was a pool which took the rainwater. The hearth, which was previously the centre of the house, was later moved to another room. As time went by, the shape of the atrium was altered to suit climatic conditions. The Roman atrium house was an autochthonous structure which, for the propertied classes, grew into a peristyle house. This peristyle usually had a garden and was surrounded by a colonnade. Great importance was attached to the design of the dining rooms and bedrooms; later additions to the house were perforce two-

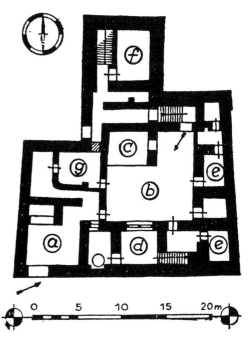

Haus in Mohenjo-Daro, aus der Wende vom 4. zum 3. Jahrtausend v. Chr.
House at Mohenjo-Daro, at the turn of the 4th to the 3rd millennium B.C.

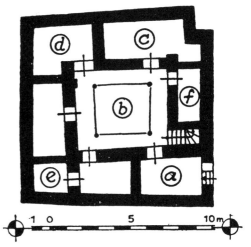

Haus in Ur (Chaldäa), aus der Wende vom 3. zum 2. Jahrtausend v. Chr.
House at Ur (Chaldea), at the turn of the 3rd to the 2nd millennium B.C.

römische Haus ausgeübt, sodass wir annehmen können, dass sich aus dem etruskischen Haus das römische Atriumhaus, als Einheitshaus mit Wohn- und Wirtschaftsräumen unter einem Dach vereint, entwickelt hat. Diese Häuser, an der Strasse aneinandergebaut, waren eingeschossig und hatten keine Fenster. Der Herd mit Rauchabzug lag im Mittelpunkt des Gebäudes, dem die Decke fehlte (Atrium). Licht kam in dieses Haus nur durch das Dach und vom Hauseingang her. Das ‹Atrium› war gewissermassen der Saal mit offenem Dach, der schliesslich die Form eines Hofes annahm. Inmitten dieses Hofes befand sich ein Becken, das das Regenwasser aufnahm. Der Herd, vorerst Mittelpunkt des Hauses, wurde später in einen anderen Raum verlegt. Die Gestalt des Atriums wurde je nach klimatischen Verhältnissen im Laufe der Zeit verändert. Das römische Atriumhaus war ein bodenständiger Typ, der sich für die Begüterten durch Erweiterung zu einem Peristylhaus entwickelte. Dieses Peristyl hatte meist einen Garten und war mit einem Säulenumgang versehen. Auf die Gestaltung der Speiseräume und Schlafräume wurde grosser Wert gelegt; später angebaute Teile des Hauses wurden aus Notwendigkeit 2geschossig gestaltet. Die Kaiserzeit des letzten Jahrhunderts vor Christi hat uns nur Reste und schriftliche Quellen hinterlassen. Nur in Pompeji und Herculanum wurden grössere Haus- und Villengruppen ausgegraben. Es ist verständlich, dass die Wohnart der Römer später in nördliche Provinzen verpflanzt wurde.

Ältere Klosteranlagen haben vom antiken Patio die Idee des Säulenhofes übernommen, ihn oft gärtnerisch geschmückt, aber ebenso oft nur mit Wasserbecken oder Brunnen versehen. Der Kreuzgang ist ein mit Bogen überwölbter Gang um den Hof, eine gedeckte Wandelhalle. Die Klöster waren in gewissem Sinne das Spiegelbild eines römischen Hauses.

storey. The imperial age, the last century before Christ, has bequeathed to us merely remains and written sources. Only in Pompeii and Herculaneum have major houses and groups of villas been excavated. It is easy to understand why the Roman style of living was later transplanted to the northern provinces. Older monastic buildings inherited the notion of the colonnaded court from the antique patio, often embellishing it with a garden, but just as often, providing it with only a pool or fountain. The cloister is an arched walk round the courtyard, a covered arcade. The monasteries were, in a certain sense, a reflection of a Roman house.

The Iraqi town house conforms to habits different from those prevailing in European courtyard houses and still reflects nomadic influences. The multistorey house has two parts, the 'divanshane' or 'selamlik' for the reception of guests and the 'haram' for the family. The house has areas which are suitable for summer and winter living, and also for the morning and evening, and consequently it is in constant use from the cellar to the roof terrace, depending on the season. One fact of special importance in the organization of family life is that no meals are eaten together. The quadrangle, usually with a pool of water, is called the 'hosh'.
This tarma house has certain affinities with the standard Pompeian plan, having a peristyle in the rear portion and furthermore a symmetrical shape. The 'livan' is the counterpart of the 'exedra', the central room corresponds to the 'oda'.
It has not so far been possible to identify the link, extending over centuries, between the tarma house and the Hellenistic house.

The Chinese house of the first century BC has changed but little over its long history. The vast majority of houses in Chinese towns are single-storeyed, access being from long straight streets.

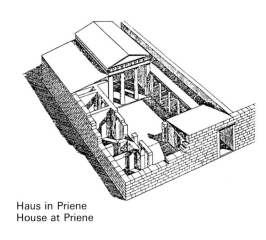

Haus in Priene
House at Priene

Patio-Haus in Ur, 2000 v. Chr.
Patio house at Ur, 2000 B.C.

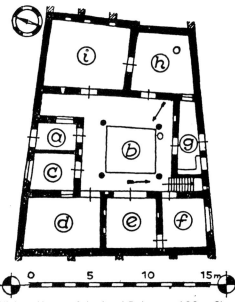

Kleines Haus auf der Insel Dalvo, ca. 100 v. Chr.
Small house on the island of Dalvo, c. 100 B.C.

Griechisches Haus, ca. 100 v. Chr.
Greek house, c. 100 B.C.

Römisches Peristylhaus
Roman peristyle house

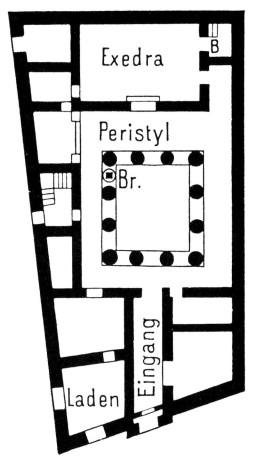

Exedra

Peristyl

Br.

Eingang

Laden

Haus auf Delos
House on Delos

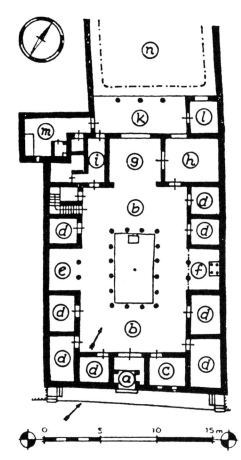

Aus der vorrömischen Zeit Pompejis,
ca. 500 v. Chr.
From the pre-Roman time of Pompeii

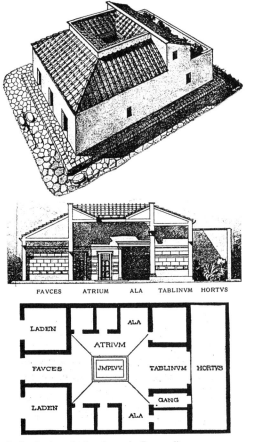

FAVCES ATRIVM ALA TABLINVM HORTVS

LADEN | ALA
FAVCES | ATRIVM | TABLINVM | HORTVS
| JMPLVV. |
LADEN | GANG
| ALA

Italienisches Atriumhaus in Pompeji
Italian atrium house at Pompeii

15

Das irakische Stadthaus wird von anderen Gewohnheiten bestimmt als europäische Hofhäuser, so sind noch vom Nomadischen her Einflüsse erkennbar. Das mehrgeschossige Haus hat zwei Teile, den ‹divanschane› oder ‹selamlik› für den Gästeverkehr, den ‹haram› für die Familie. Das Haus bietet ausserdem für den Sommer und den Winteraufenthalt, auch für morgens und abends gute Plätze, es wird daher je nach Jahreszeit vom Keller bis zur Dachterrasse benützt. Ein wesentliches Moment innerhalb der Familie ist, dass keine gemeinsamen Mahlzeiten eingenommen werden. Der quadratische Hof, meist mit Wasserbecken, wird ‹hosch› genannt.

Dieses Tarmahaus hat eine gewisse Verwandtschaft mit dem pompejianischen Normalgrundriss, mit dem im hinteren Teil befindlichen Peristyl: es zeigt ausserdem symmetrische Ausbildung. Der ‹livan› entspricht der ‹exedra›, dem Mittelraum als ‹oda›.

Bisher konnte die Jahrhunderte betreffende Lücke der Entwicklung vom Tarmahaus zum hellenistischen Haus nicht nachgewiesen werden.

Das chinesische Haus im ersten Jahrhundert vor Christus hat sich in der langen Geschichte wenig verändert. Chinesische Städte haben überwiegend ebenerdige Häuser, die von geraden Strassen aufgeschlossen sind. Es handelt sich fast immer um ein Pavillonsystem, das bedeutet, dass die den Hof umgebenden Bauten Einzelhäuser sind, die jedoch zu einem Ganzen zusammengesetzt werden. Diese Anordnung konnte entsprechend der Familienstruktur der Chinesen nach der Rückseite durch neue Höfe mit ihren Häusern für Söhne und Verwandte erweitert werden: es entstand dadurch eine Art Teppichsiedlung. Drei Stufen hinauf sind am Eingang zum Haus angelegt, dann ein Pförtnerzimmer, dahinter ein kleiner Eingangshof und links meist ein Vorhof mit Empfangsräumen oder dem Arbeitszimmer des Hausherrn. Der Hof selbst

In almost every case there is a pavilion system, that is to say, the buildings enclosing the courtyard are single houses, which are, however, composed into a whole. To meet the exigencies of Chinese family life, this arrangement can be extended to the rear by new courtyards with their houses for sons and relations, resulting in a kind of 'cellular' development. There are three steps leading up into the house, then a porter's room, behind which is a small entrance courtyard and, to the left, usually a forecourt with reception rooms or the master's study. The courtyard itself is invariably a garden courtyard with covered verandas, single trees and large flower tubs with oleander and pomegranate trees. Concepts such as tree, flower, water and mountain are represented symbolically – a world in miniature. For Europeans this house is always a model, often down to the details.

In the Chinese house, the wall opposite the entrance known as the 'shadow wall' – its purpose is to keep out evil spirits – provides the desired privacy, making the courtyard an oasis of tranquillity. The pillared walks in front of the pavilion with their red wooden columns bring movement and rest into contrast. Some of these examples will demonstrate the various types of house.

In Europe courtyard houses were the creation of the cramped conditions and upward building made necessary by defence needs and this had its effect on the form of the courtyard. A large number of inhabitants had to be accommodated within small spaces inside the medieval town. There are many kinds of inner courtyards with surrounding walls, sometimes pillared walks; particularly good examples can be seen in Salzburg, Steyr and Vienna. Until 1900 there were 128 courtyards in Vienna. They originated from ecclesiastical and also lay households or were private courtyards round which a number of houses were grouped. Later, in the

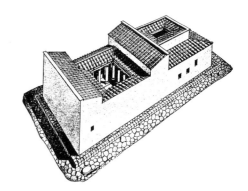

Italienisches Haus mit Peristyl
Italian house with peristyle

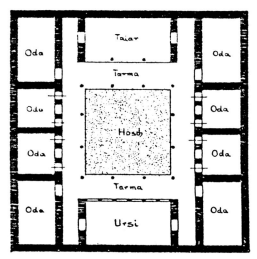

Idealplan für einen quadratischen Hof (Musterplan eines Tarmahausschemas)
Ideal plan for a quadrangular court (model plan of a tarma house layout)

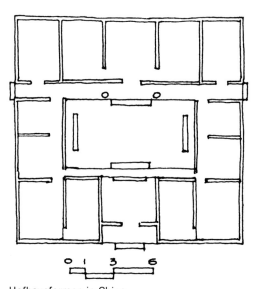

Hofhausformen in China
Forms of courtyard house in China

Traditionelles Hofhaus in Beijing
Traditional courtyard house in Beijing

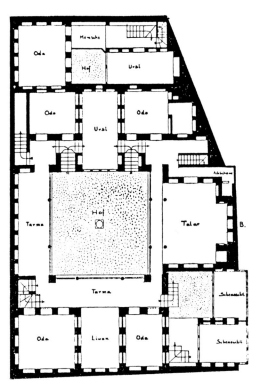

Haus des Murad Effendi, Hilleh, Grundriss des Obergeschosses.
House of the Murad Effendi, Hilleh, plan of the upper floor

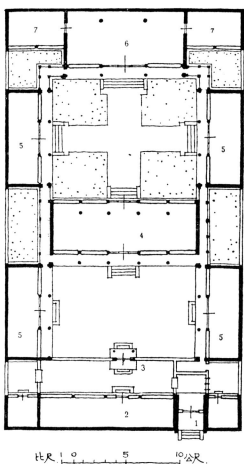

Typisches Hu-t'ung (kleines Alleehaus) in Beijing
Typical Hu-t'ung (small alley house) in Beijing

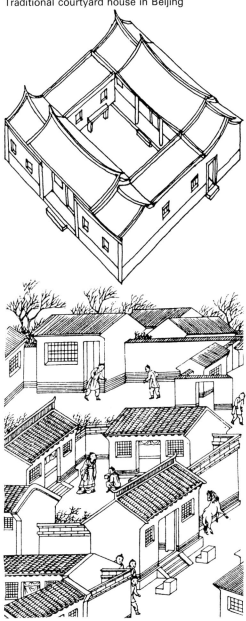

Siedlung mit Wohngehöften um 1900, China
Settlement with homesteads, c. 1900, China

ist immer ein Gartenhof mit gedeckten Veranden, einzelnen Bäumen und grossen Blumenkübeln mit Oleander- und Granatbäumen. Symbolisch werden Begriffe wie Baum, Blume, Wasser, Berg dargestellt, eine Welt im Kleinen. Dieses Haus bildete für Europäer immer schon ein Vorbild, oft bis in Details. Im chinesischen Haus bildet die sogenannte Schattenmauer gegenüber dem Eingang – die die schlechten Geister abhalten soll – auch den gewünschten Intimbereich, sie schafft Ruhe für den Hof. Die dem Pavillon vorgelagerten überdeckten Säulengänge mit ihren roten Holzsäulen bilden den Gegensatz von Bewegung und Ruhe. Einige dieser Beispiele wollen die verschiedenen Haustypen demonstrieren.

In Europa entstanden Wohnhöfe bedingt durch die Enge der zu verteidigenden Stadt. Dies, und die notwendige Höhenentwicklung der Häuser, haben sich auf die Hofform ausgewirkt. Es war der Zwang, auf kleinen Räumen innerhalb der mittelalterlichen Stadt viele Bewohner unterzubringen. Innenhöfe mit Umgängen, auch Säulenumgängen versehen, gibt es in vielen Varianten, besonders gute Beispiele davon in Salzburg, Steyr und Wien. Bis um 1900 gab es in Wien 128 Höfe. Sie stammten aus kirchlichen und weltlichen Hofhaltungen oder waren private Höfe, um die sich mehrere Höfe gruppierten. Später, in den zwanziger Jahren dieses Jahrhunderts, entstanden mit dem grossen Sozialprogramm der Gemeinde Wien eine Reihe von ‹Höfen›, von denen einige berechtigt den Namen ‹Superblock› tragen. Alle diese bekannten Bauten tragen den Namen ‹Hof›. Bereits in der Zeit des Historismus im vorigen Jahrhundert wurde diese Bezeichnung für grosse Gebäudeanlagen, u.a. für den ‹Heinrichshof› (von Th. Hansen) gewählt. Bischöfe und geistliche Würdenträger hatten mit grossen Mitteln Baulichkeiten angekauft und zu Stiftshöfen adaptiert (‹Heiligenkreuzerhof›, ‹Melcherhof›). Der Anlass zu diesen

twenties of this century, the large-scale social housing schemes of the City of Vienna produced a number of 'Courts', some of which merit the name of 'superblocks'. All these well-known buildings have the name 'Hof' (Court). Even during the historicist period of the preceding century, this name was bestowed on large complexes of buildings, as for example the 'Heinrichshof' (by Th. Hansen). Bishops and church dignitaries had spent large sums of money on buying properties and adapting them to 'Stiftshöfe' ('Heiligenkreuzhof', 'Melcherhof'). The purpose of these was to provide comfortable accommodation. These ecclesiastical courts were the model for the imperial palace complex whereas the private courtyards mainly served as branch establishments for mercantile interests. ('Regensburgerhof'). Constructions of this kind began with Rudolf von Habsburg and have continued down to the present day. Characteristic examples are the 'Renaissancehof', the 'Grabenhof', 1476, the 'Federlhof', 1590, where, among others, Wallenstein and later Leibnitz lived. Some of the suburban courtyard houses built in the Biedermeier style have survived down to the present and radiate their charming musicality. It is hardly surprising that Schubert was born in such a courtyard house and Beethoven lived successively in a number of them. These houses have an elongated courtyard with sometimes external staircases giving access to the upper floor, as well as walks along the courtyard side with fine grilles and roof cornices consisting of concave mouldings. In the paved yard stands a fountain; trees used to be trained on wall espaliers.
The houses of the Burgenland type in small towns have a courtyard abutting on the house next door that usually presents a high wall, and, on the right or left side, a house running far back with windows overlooking the court, which is a working yard. Only one room has a window on the street; the house is

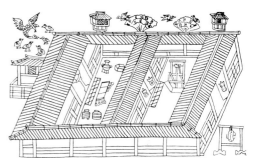

Wohngehöft aus der Han-Zeit, China
Dwelling house from the Han dynasty, China

Hof des Amerlinghauses am Spittelberg, Wien
Courtyard of the Amerlinghaus on the Spittelberg, Vienna

Hof des Bürgerspitals in der Wiener Neustadt
Courtyard of the Citizens' Hospital in Wiener
Neustadt

Beethovens Wohnhaus in Heiligenstadt, Wien
Beethoven's house at Heiligenstadt, Vienna

Hof in Nussdorf, Wien
Courtyard at Nussdorf, Vienna

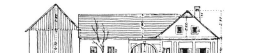

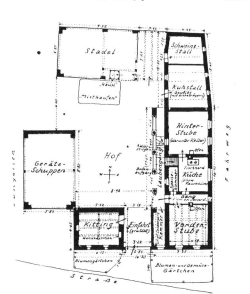

Bauernhaus in Oberschützen mit Laubengang,
Südburgenland
Farmhouse at Oberschützen with loggia,
Südburgenland

Hof des Schubert-Geburtshauses an der Nussdorf-
strasse, Wien
Courtyard of the house in the Nussdorfstrasse,
Vienna, where Schubert was born

sen Unternehmungen war, bequeme Absteigequartiere zu schaffen. Die Prälatenhöfe waren Vorbild auch für die kaiserlichen Anlagen, während die privaten Höfe meist kaufmännischen Interessen für Niederlassungen («Regensburgerhof») dienten. Diese Art der Anlagen beginnt mit Rudolf von Habsburg und dauert bis in unsere Zeit. Charakteristische Beispiele sind der «Renaissancehof», der «Grabenhof», 1476, der «Federlhof», 1590, in dem u.a. Wallenstein und später Leibnitz wohnten. Die biedermeierlichen Vorstadthaushöfe aber haben sich zum Teil bis in die Gegenwart erhalten und strahlen mit ihrer reizvollen Art Musikalität aus. Es ist daher nicht zu verwundern, dass Schubert in einem solchen Hof geboren wurde und Beethoven in verschiedenen dieser Höfe gewohnt hat. Diese Häuser haben einen länglichen Hof; manchmal führen äussere Treppen ins obere Geschoss sowie Pawlatschengänge mit feinen Stabgittern und weit vorspringenden Dachgesimsen, die als Hohlkehlen ausgebildet sind. Im gepflasterten Hof befindet sich ein Brunnen; Spalierbäume werden an den Hauswänden gezogen.

Die burgenländischen Haustypen der kleinen Orte haben zum Nachbarhaus, das meist mit einer hohen Wand abschloss, einen Hof und auf der rechten oder linken Seite ein tiefes Haus mit Fenstern auf diesen Wirtschaftshof. Nur ein Zimmer hat Fenster auf die Strasse, das Haus wird durch das grosse Tor, das auch Einfahrt ist, betreten. Die Wiener Vorstadthäuser haben diesen Haustyp übernommen, mit einem winkelförmigen oder U-förmigen Hausschema. Viele dieser Häuser sind ganz oder teilweise zweigeschossig und haben manchmal einen verglasten Gang, im Volksmund «Pawlatsche» genannt. Ein hervorragendes Beispiel, das viel Musikalität ausstrahlt, ist Schuberts Geburtshaus in Wien, Nussdorferstrasse, das alle Merkmale dieser Zeit in sich vereint. Dieses Haus hat einen U-förmigen Grundriss, bei dem

entered by the big gate which is also a carriage-gate. This style was taken over for the suburban houses of Vienna, which are built on an L-shaped or U-shaped layout. Many of these houses are two-storeyed throughout or in parts and sometimes have a glazed walk round the courtyard, known locally as a 'Pawlatsche'. An outstanding example, which radiates a great deal of musicality, is Schubert's birthplace in Vienna, Nussdorferstrasse, where all the features of this period are united. This house has a U-shaped plan, the fourth side being a garden, separated from the courtyard by a paling. The upper storey is reached by two staircases, the landings of which are pillared. The walk above the entrance is glazed. Another example is the house where Beethoven died, the 'Schwarzspanierhaus', which also had a large courtyard (built by immigrant Benedictine monks.) Beethoven's house in Baden bears a close resemblance to Schubert's birthplace. (Also houses where Beethoven lived in Mödling and Heiligenstadt.)

The great Baroque monasteries in Austria and Bavaria possessed a number of courtyards within the building complex. One of the most beautiful of these is in Kremsmünster – the 'Fischkalter' as it is called – consisting of a succession of courtyards with pools of water and covered walks. Another example is the courtyard of the chapter house at the monastery St. Florian in Upper Austria, the staircase of which, by its external design, strikes a dominant note in the courtyard. During the Baroque age the many large monasteries with their tranquil courtyards exercised a great influence on secular buildings. Indeed, it would not be too much to say that the classic rectangular courtyard of Austria, growing from this heritage, reached an acme of perfection. This book on the courtyard house would not be complete without some reference to farm courtyards. The 'Vierkant' (square) is an Upper Austrian farmhouse in the best wheat-growing area

Hof des Beethovenhauses in Baden
Courtyard of the Beethoven house at Baden

die vierte Seite der Garten einnimmt, der mit einem Gitterzaun vom Hof abgeschlossen ist. Das Obergeschoss erreicht man über zwei Treppen, deren Podeste Säulen tragen. Über der Einfahrt ist der Gang verglast. Ein anderes Beispiel ist Beethovens Sterbehaus, das sogenannte ‹Schwarzspanierhaus›, das auch einen grossen Hof hat (von eingewanderten Benediktinern erbaut). Beethovens Wohnhaus in Baden zeigt eine grosse Ähnlichkeit mit Schuberts Geburtshaus. (Beethovenhaus in Mödling und Heiligenstadt.)

Die grossen Barockklöster in Österreich und Bayern hatten ganze Reihen von Höfen innerhalb der Baukomplexe. Einer der schönsten Höfe ist in Kremsmünster – der sogenannte ‹Fischkalter›, eine mit Wasserbecken und überdeckten Wandelgängen ausgebildete Hoffolge. Ein anderes Beispiel, da wir eine grosse Zahl kennen, ist der Hof des Stiftes St. Florian in Oberösterreich, dessen Treppenhaus durch seine äussere Gestaltung dem Hof Dominanz verleiht. Im Barockzeitalter haben die vielen grossen Klosteranlagen mit ihren stillen Höfen grosse Wirkung auf Profanbauten ausgeübt, ja man könnte behaupten, dass der klassische Vierkanthof Oberösterreichs sich aus diesem Gedankengut zu einer vollkommenen Form entwickelt hat.

Diese Abhandlung über das Hofhaus wäre unvollständig, würde man nicht die bäuerlichen Hofformen in diese kurze Untersuchung miteinbeziehen. Der ‹Vierkant› ist ein oberösterreichisches Bauernhaus in der Gegend der besten Weizenböden und bildet eine vollendete Hofform in technisch-organisatorischer Hinsicht, und ist daher ein Höhepunkt bäuerlicher Gehöftformen. Erste Höfe dieser Art sind um 1649 im ‹Merian› ersichtlich. Trotz vieler Abarten blieb er aber ein allgemeiner Formtyp, in dem vier Gebäude zu einem Ganzen verschmelzen mit scharfen Kanten und einem Dach mit vier Graten. Der grosse Hofraum von quadratischer Form ist vollständig geschlossen und umgürtet

and, from the organizational and technical point of view, might be described as the last word in courtyard layout. The first farms of this kind can be seen c. 1649 in 'Merian'. In spite of many variants, it has remained a general model in which four buildings are amalgamated in a pattern with sharp edges and a four-ridged roof. A large square yard is completely shut in, the enclosure thus being effected with a minimum of walls or roofs. The walls are sometimes of raw brickwork and sometimes they are rendered white. The original roofing was of thatch on steeply sloping rafters. The 'Vierkant' is a single farmhouse with a living room which almost always looks to the south while the kitchen faces north. An elevated paved walk runs round two or three sides of the yard.

The 'Vierseithof', as the name implies, has four sides and likewise has a square yard. It is still often constructed as a timber building and differs from the 'Vierkant' in the construction of the roof and particularly in its pitch, which is not so steep on the house as on the stable and barns. In one corner the living quarters are concentrated. In earlier times the scattered farmstead was the usual form. The farmhouse is always built of wood. The various links between the buildings are often richly decorated board fences or walls pierced by large entrance gates. The centre of the yard was originally the dung heap and the liquid manure pit.

In the 'Dreiseithof' the rectangular yard is enclosed only on three sides and the fourth side has a wall or a wooden fence and gate. This form is typical of regions where little corn is grown. It is also found in closely built row villages. The yard is almost always rectangular and elongated.

Among the many designs produced by Josef Frank there are several plans for atrium houses which have never been executed. Josef Frank could therefore be said to have been a convinced 'court-

Vierkanthof, Oberösterreich
'Vierkanthof', farmhouse in Upper Austria

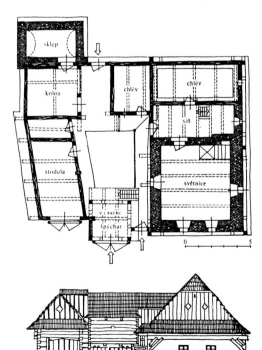

Slowakisches Hofhaus in Borowá u Policky
Slovakian courtyard house at Borowá u Policky

so mit einem Minimum an Mauern und Dachflächen. Er zeigt manchmal die rohen Ziegel oder ist weiss verputzt. Die ursprüngliche Deckung aber war ein Strohdach auf steilgestellten Sparren. Der ‹Vierkant› ist ein Einzelhof, dessen Wohnstube fast immer nach Süden gerichtet ist, die Küche aber nach Norden. Ein erhöhter, gepflasterter Gang führt im Hof an zwei oder drei Seiten herum.

Der ‹Vierseithof› baut sich auch aus vier Seiten auf und hat ebenso einen quadratischen Hof. Noch oft als Holzbau ausgeführt, unterscheidet er sich zum Vierkanthof in der Dachkonstruktion und Dachneigung, die am Wohnhaus geringer ist als bei Stall und Scheunen. An einer Ecke ist die Anlage dann zu einem Ganzen verbunden. Frühere Formen zeigen den lose verbundenen Haufenhof. Das Wohnhaus ist immer aus Holz gezimmert. Die verschiedenen Verbindungsglieder der Baukörper sind als Bretterwände oft reich verziert oder als Mauern mit grossen Einfahrtstoren ausgeführt. Das Zentrum des Hofes war ursprünglich der Misthaufen und die Jauchegrube.

Am ‹Dreiseithof› (auch fränkisches Gehöft) ist der viereckige Hofraum nur an drei Seiten umbaut, die vierte Seite wird mit Mauer oder Holzwand, Tor geschlossen. Diese Hofform stammt aus Gegenden mit geringem Getreideanbau. Man trifft diesen Typus auch in geschlossen gebauten Reihendörfern. Der Hofraum ist fast immer langgezogen und rechteckig.

Josef Frank hat unter vielen Entwürfen mehrere Atriumhäuser geplant, von denen aber keines ausgeführt wurde. Man könnte daher behaupten, Josef Frank sei ein überzeugter ‹Hofhausarchitekt› gewesen. Vom vollkommen umschlossenen Hof bis teilweise auch unregelmässig umschlossenen Höfen reicht sein Entwurfsspektrum. Sie sind der beste Beweis für die Lebendigkeit des Gedankens für das zeitgemässe Patiohaus und seine immerwährende

yard house architect'. His designs range from the completely to the partly and sometimes irregularly enclosed courtyard. They are the best testimony to the vitality of the thought informing the contemporary patio house and its relevance to present-day conditions. The project for a country house M.S. for Los Angeles, of which three variant forms exist, shows how Josef Frank's mind worked on the subject of the courtyard house. They date back to the nineteen-twenties. In the first design Josef Frank gave the elongated courtyard a curved shape with a longish pool of water in the curve, also a double flight of steps negotiating the difference in level inside the house. The patio court is designed on the lines of Japanese gardens. The house and courtyard continuum is particularly enlivened by this unconventional shape; Josef Frank's second version to suit the Californian climate is built on an almost square plan. A single-storey house is integrated into the surrounding landscape by projections and setbacks of spaces and parts of spaces. This creates the illusion of a large ramified house with many rooms and differentiated spatial grouping, and this is intensified by the six steps leading to the bedroom wing. The centre, as usual, is the patio garden. The house No. 10 for Mrs Dagmar Grill is one of the simple house designs with a patio, dating from the late period after 1945. It is built up on a rectangular plan with a living and dining room enclosing the atrium. In the south of the room there is an additional oriel-like extension. The large covered terrace is approached from the living room; above, there are three bedrooms with a roof terrace. Even in this relatively small house, Josef Frank's spatial mastery is surprising. The Strnad-Schule (School of Applied Arts Vienna), through Erich Boltenstern, published in 1934 'The Home for Everyone', representing the work done by one particular class. In its pages a courtyard designed for living in is shown. This version illustrates how, by

Nordmühlviertler Dreiseithof
'Dreiseithof', farmhouse in Nordmühlviertl

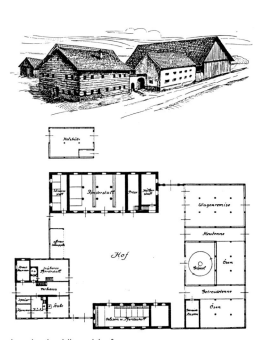

Innviertler Vierseithof
'Vierseithof', farmhouse in Innviertl

Aktualität. Das Projekt eines Landhauses M.S. für Los Angeles, von dem es drei Varianten gibt, zeigen die Gedankengänge Josef Franks für das Thema Hofhaus. Sie stammen aus den späten zwanziger Jahren. Im ersten Entwurf hat Josef Frank den langgestreckten Hof gekrümmt, dem in der Krümmung ein längliches Wasserbecken folgt, ebenso eine zweiarmige Treppe, welche die Höhendifferenz innerhalb des Hauses überwindet. Der Patiohof ist ähnlich den japanischen Gärten gestaltet. Die Verbindung Haus – Hof wird durch diese eigenwillige Form besonders intensiv und lebendig: Josef Franks zweite Version für das kalifornische Klima ist fast auf einem Quadrat aufgebaut. Ein ebenerdiges Wohnhaus ist durch Rück- und Vorsprünge von Räumen oder Raumteilen in die umgebende Landschaft integriert. Dadurch entsteht die Illusion eines weitverzweigten, grossen Hauses mit vielen Räumen und differenzierten Raumgruppen, die durch den Höhenunterschied von sechs Stufen zum Schlaftrakt noch gesteigert wird. Mittelpunkt bildet aber wie immer der Patiogarten.

Das Haus D Nr. 10 für Frau Dagmar Grill ist einer der einfachen Hausentwürfe mit Patio aus der Spätzeit nach 1945. Es ist auf einem rechteckigen Grundriss aufgebaut mit einem grossen, das Atrium umschliessenden Living- and Diningroom. Dieser hat im Süden eine zusätzliche erkerartige Erweiterung. Die grosse, überdeckte Terrasse ist vom Livingroom aufgeschlossen, darüber befinden sich drei Schlafräume mit Dachterrasse. Auch an diesem einfachen Haus überrascht das grosse räumliche Wegkonzept Josef Franks. Die Strnad-Schule (Kunstgewerbeschule Wien) publizierte 1934 durch Erich Boltenstern eine Klassenarbeit ‹Die Wohnung für Jedermann›. In dieser ist ein Wohnhof mit Wohnraum dargestellt. Diese Version zeigt, wie durch zarte Bepflanzung mit sparsamen Möbeln eine phantasievolle Weiterent-

sensitive placing of the furniture, it is possible to produce an imaginative continuation of the Biedermeier house which is still classical in appearance. Lois Welzenbacher, an architect who has converted the sculptural quality of his south Tyrolean houses into country houses for urban dwellers of our age, has shown two examples of houses with open inner courts. These houses were built about 1940. One is in Cröllwitz-Halle near Munich and Welzenbacher's sketch clearly brings out its integration into the loosely arranged building layout. In the other example the house is situated in a mountainous landscape and is grouped round a forecourt. In its design it recalls solid old farmhouses while remaining free from folkloric overtones.

The villa 'Savoye in Poisy', designed by Le Corbusier and built c. 1929, is an unusual example of a courtyard house. The upper floor, standing on delicate pillars, also serves as a living floor, and has an enclosed courtyard garden, which might be described as a roof garden.

The living rooms look over this courtyard terrace, which is closed on one side by a window wall. A clerestorey of sliding windows runs round all facades. The courtyard, which is intended to be lived in, is partly planted and has a ramp leading up to the solarium and the roof superstructures.

After 1945 there was a marked tendency to plan urban dwelling houses (private houses) as garden courtyard houses in the form of 'cellular' settlements.

There is no doubt that Chinese and Ottoman examples can be a useful guide in the development of low profile houses, for they have certain features which fit well into our present habits. In old Ottoman houses the internal layout, the comfort afforded by the sedia running along the walls, and the many verandas or balcony-like projections directly related to the garden and the house make a convincing design.

Entwurf eines Landhauses in Los Angeles von Josef Frank, 1930
Design for a country house in Los Angeles by Josef Frank, 1930

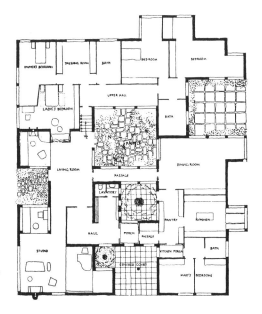

Zweiter Entwurf des Landhauses von Josef Frank, 1930
Second design for the country house by Josef Frank, 1930

wicklung des Biedermeierhauses möglich ist und dabei klassisch wirkt.

Lois Welzenbacher, ein Architekt, der die plastische Wirkung seiner Südtiroler Häuser in Landhäuser für städtische Bewohner unserer Zeit umgesetzt hat, hat zwei Beispiele für Holzhäuser mit offenem Innenhof gezeigt. Diese Häuser entstanden um 1940, von denen das eine in Cröllwitz-Halle bei München steht und durch die Handskizze Welzenbachers besonders gut die Einbindung in die aufgelockerte Bauanlage zeigt. Im anderen Beispiel steht das Haus in einer gebirgigen Landschaft und ist um einen Vorhof gruppiert, es erinnert durch seine Gestaltung an gute alte Bauernhäuser, ohne dass wir von einer Folklorearchitektur sprechen können.

Die von Le Corbusier entworfene Villa ‹Savoye in Poisy›, um 1929 gebaut, ist ein besonderes Beispiel eines Hofhauses. Das auf zarten Säulen schwebende Obergeschoss, auch Wohngeschoss, hat einen umschlossenen Gartenhof, man könnte auch sagen Dachgartenhof.

Die Wohnräume sind auf diese Hofterrasse gerichtet, die an einer Seite durch eine Fensterwand abgeschlossen ist. Ein Schiebefensterband umzieht alle Fassaden. Der Hof ist ein richtiger Wohnhof mit teilweiser Bepflanzung und einem Rampensteg zum Solarium und den Dachaufbauten.

Nach 1945 gab es eine starke Tendenz, als städtisches Wohnhaus (Einfamilienhaus) Gartenhofhäuser in Form von Teppichsiedlungen zu planen.

Es ist sicher, dass uns chinesische und osmanische Beispiele für die Entwicklung der niederen Häuser weiterhelfen könnten, haben sie doch einige Aspekte, die auf unsere gegenwärtigen Gewohnheiten gut passen. Alte osmanische Häuser überzeugen durch ihre Lösung für das Innere des Hauses, mit ihrer Bequemlichkeit durch die an den Mauern entlang führende Sedia; viele Veranden oder balkonartige Vorsprünge stehen in direkter Beziehung zu Garten und Wohnung.

Unter den vielen Entwürfen von James

Of the many designs produced by James Stirling in the fifties, one for a courtyard house is of particular interest in this context. Using prefabricated elements and a unit construction system, he wanted to design a house that could increase and decrease in size. The house, arranged round a patio and one storey in height, could grow into a two-storey building or later be reduced in size again. Most of the rooms are disposed round the courtyard. This house is of interest because, although prefabricated in construction, it does aim at a certain romanticism.

American atrium houses of the last fifty years show architectural thinking in which antique patio houses and present living habits and technical structures are amalgamated – only the idea of the garden court from the early years of the classical atrium house appears to have been retained. Yet new attempts are always being made, whether in the form of 'cellular' settlements with L-shaped houses or whole clusters of houses enclosing the courtyard, as in Germany, Sweden and Italy. The types referred to in this short account pertain not only to single-storey courtyard houses, as in other publications, but also to multistorey structures, which may be of importance for the future development of the city.

Farmhouses with courtyards, which have been mentioned by way of example, show the multiformity of a development which is linked with our age-old patterns of behaviour.

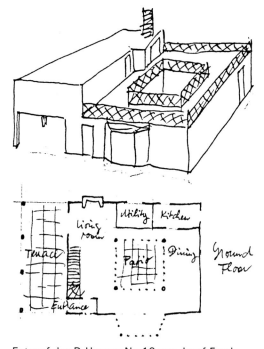

Entwurf des D-Hauses Nr. 10 von Josef Frank, 1947
Design of the D house, No. 10, by Josef Frank, 1947

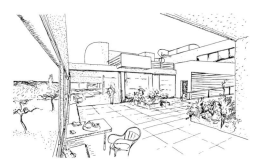

Projekt eines Wohnhofes aus der Strnad-Klasse
der Kunstgewerbeschule, Wien, 1933
Project for a courtyard house by the Strnad class
of the College of Applied Arts, Vienna, 1933

Skizze eines Hauses mit Hof in Cröllwitz-Halle b.
München von Lois Welzenbacher
Sketch of a house with courtyard at Cröllwitz-Halle,
near Munich, by Lois Welzenbacher

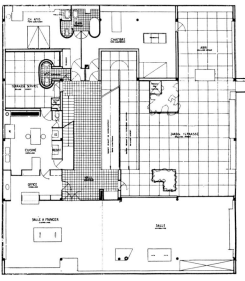

Villa Savoye, Obergeschoss und Wohnhof von
Le Corbusier, 1929
Villa Savoye, upper floor and courtyard by
Le Corbusier, 1929

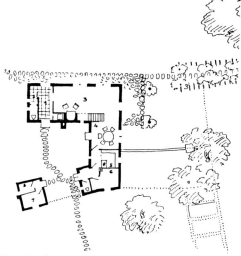

Haus in Obergrainau von Lois Welzenbacher
House at Obergrainau by Lois Welzenbacher

Stirling aus den fünfziger Jahren ist
einer, ein Hofhaus betreffend, in diesem Zusammenhang interessant. Er
wollte aus vorgefertigten Elementen
nach einem Baukastensystem ein
wachsendes bzw. schrumpfendes
Haus gestalten, ein Haus, das um einen
Patio aus einem Erdgeschosshaus zu
einer zweigeschossigen Anlage wächst,
oder später wieder schrumpft. Die mei-
sten Räume sind auf diesen Hof gerichtet. Dieses Haus ist deshalb interessant,
weil es trotz des Fertighauscharakters
eine gewisse Romantik anstrebt.
Amerikanische Hofhäuser aus den letzten fünfzig Jahren zeigen eine ideelle
Umsetzung der antiken Patiohäuser
mit gegenwärtigen Wohngewohnheiten
und technischem Aufbau – es scheint
nur der Gedanke des Gartenhofes aus
der Frühzeit des klassischen Atrium-
hauses verblieben zu sein. Trotzdem
wird immer wieder experimentiert, ob
nun in Form von Teppichsiedlungen mit
Winkelhäusern oder ganzen, den Hof
umschliessenden Gruppen von Häusern
wie in Deutschland, Schweden und Ita-
lien. Die in dieser kurzen Schrift
erwähnten Typen betreffen nicht nur
wie in anderen Veröffentlichungen
ebenerdige Hofhäuser, sondern auch
mehrgeschossige, die für die zukünftige
Entwicklung der Stadt Bedeutung
haben könnten.
Die bäuerlichen Hofhäuser, die als Beispiel gezeigt werden, beweisen die Vielfalt einer Entwicklung, die mit unseren
urtümlichen Verhaltensweisen im
Zusammenhang steht.

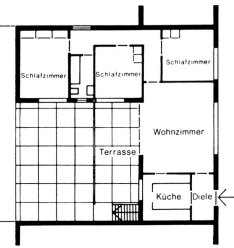

Wohnhaus in der Werkbundsiedlung in Wien, von
Anton Brenner, 1932
House in the Werkbundsiedlung in Vienna, by
Anton Brenner, 1932

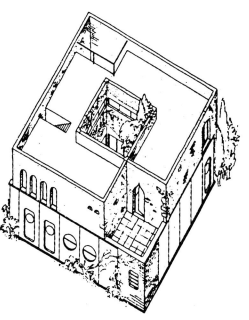

Entwurf eines Wohnhauses in Salzburg von Josef
Frank, 1926
Design for a house at Salzburg by Josef Frank,
1926

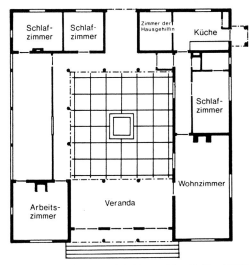

Atriumhaus Oivala, Helsinki, von Oiva Kallio, 1925
Atrium house Oivala, Helsinki, by Oiva Kallio, 1925

Wachsendes, bzw. schrumpfendes Haus mit Hof
aus vorgefertigten Elementen von James Stirling,
1957
House of prefabricated elements, with courtyard,
designed to be adaptable in size, by James Stirling,
1957

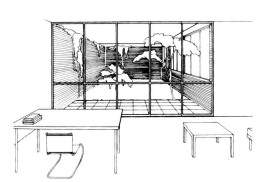

Hofhausprojekt am Bauhaus von Eduard Ludwig,
1932–33
Courtyard house project at the Bauhaus by Eduard
Ludwig, 1932–33

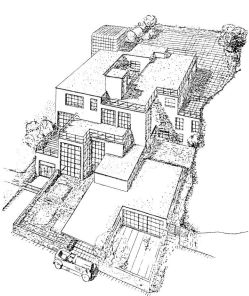

Entwurf eines Wohnhauses in Pasadena,
(Kalifornien), von Josef Frank, 1927
Design for a house at Pasadena (California), by
Josef Frank, 1927

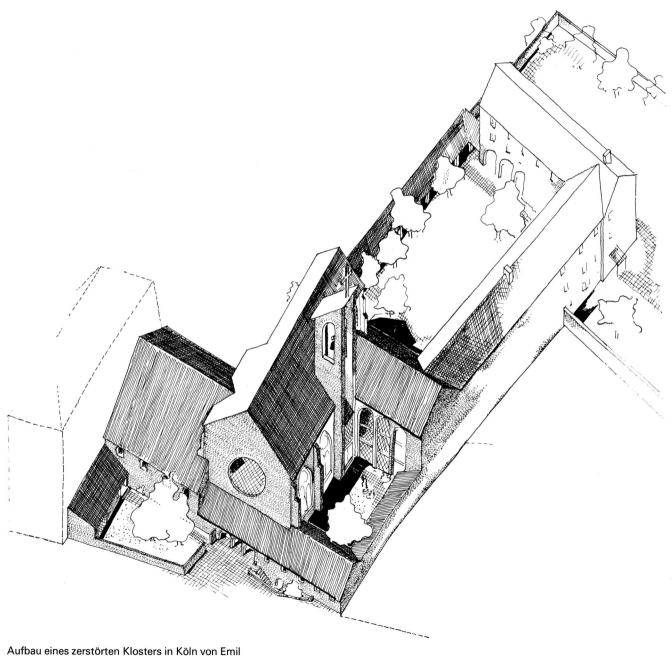

Aufbau eines zerstörten Klosters in Köln von Emil
Steffan, 1947–51.

Reconstruction of a ruined monastery in Cologne
by Emil Steffan, 1947–51.

Literatur/Bibliography

Wiener Höfe einst und jetzt, Margarete Girardi, Verlag Ernst Müller, Wien 1947

Gartenhofhäuser, Duncan Macintosh, Deutsche Verlagsanstalt, Stuttgart 1973

Kleine Weltgeschichte des städtischen Wohnhauses, Ludolf Veltheim-Lottum, Verlag Lambert Schneider, Heidelberg 1952

Der animale Weg, Fred Fischer, Verlag für Architektur Artemis, Zürich 1972

La maison chinoise, Liu Dunzhen, Architectures Bibliothèque Berger-Levrault 1980

Arbeiten von Lois Welzenbacher, Moderne Bauformen, XLI Heft 9, Sept. 1942

Der traditionelle Holzwohnbau im östlichen Schwarzmeer-Gebiet – Probleme der Integration in zeitgenössische Architektur, Dissertation von Fikret Evci, Istanbul, Techn. Univ. Wien 1981

Das Wohnhaus in Bagdad und anderen Städten des Irak, Dissertation von Dr. Ing. Oskar Reuther, Techn. Hochschule Dresden, Verlag Ernst Wasmuth A.G., Berlin 1910

A Survey of Kinmen Traditional Architecture, Lee Chien-Lang, Printed in Taipei 1978

Anonymes Bauen – Westöstlicher Divan, Sokratis Dimitriou, und Anonymes Bauen in Mittel- und Ostpersien, Material und Konstruktion, Hasso Homann, in Bauforum 44, 7. Jg. 1974, Baufachverlag Wien, Ges.m.b.H.

Peking, Margarete Schütte-Lihotzky, in «der aufbau» 2, 1958, Stadtbauamt Wien

Das chinesische Wohnhaus, Rudolf Kelling, Tokyo 1935, Deutsche Gesellschaft für Natur und Völkerkunde Ostasiens

Alt-Wiener Musikstätten, Karl Kobald, Amalthea Verlag 1919, Zürich, Leipzig, Wien

Das antike griechisch-römische Wohnhaus, Walter Lange, Leipzig 1878, Verlag von G. Knapp

Oberösterreichische Baufibel, Rudolf Heckl, Otto Müller Verlag, Salzburg 1949

In alten Bauernhäusern leben, Herrad Spielhofer, Leopold Stocker Verlag, Graz 1980

Lebende Tradition, Ilse Luger, ÖLV-Buchverlag – Oberösterr. Landesverlag 1981

Josef Frank, von Johannes Spalt und Hermann Czech, Hochschule für Angewandte Kunst, Wien 1981

Atriumhäuser, Paulhans Peters, Verlag Georg D.W. Callwey, München

Bauen in Holz, Hans Stolper

Die Wohnung für jedermann, Julius Hoffmann Verlag, Stuttgart 1933

China II. Band, Bernd Melchers, Folkwang Verlag G.m.b.H., Hagen i.W. 1922

Chinese Architecture, Andrew Boyd, London, Alec Tiranti 1962

Mensch und Raum, Otto Friedrich Bollnow, W. Kohlhammer Verlag, Stuttgart, Berlin, Köln, Mainz 1963

Kleine Einfamilienhäuser, H.A. Vetter, Verlag Anton Schroll & Co. in Wien 1932

Wiener Häuser, Hartwig Fischel, 1. Teil, Benjamin Harz Verlag, Berlin, Wien 1923

Kunst und Leben im Altertum, Hugo Muzik und Franz Perschinka, F. Thupsky, Wien, G. Freytag, Leipzig 1909

Geschichte des Städtebaues, 1. und 2. Band von Ernst Egli, Eugen Rentsch Verlag, Zürich 1962

Bäuerliche Bauten im Südburgenland, Franz Simon, Selbstverlag 1971

Die Alhambra und der Generalife, Führer von Marino Antequera, Ediciones Miguel Sanchez, Granada

Tadao Ando, Prolgomena, Katalog der Ausstellung in Wien 1985

Die Stellung des bosnischen Hauses, Dr. Rudolf Mehringer 1909

Das Bauernhaus in Oberösterreich, Dr. Eduard Kriechbaum, J. Engelhorns Nachfolger in Stuttgart 1933

Gestörte Idyllen, Jens Tismar, Walter Müller, Karl Hanser Verlag 1973, München

Klassische chinesische Baukunst, Thomas Thilo, Edition Tusch, Wien 1977

Anonymes Bauen im Iran, Roland Rainer, Akad. Druck- und Verlagsanstalt, Graz 1977

Das türkische Wohnhaus, in: «La Turquie Kamaliste» Seite 11, Heft Nr. 14/1936

Le Corbusier, 1910–1929, Edition Girsberger, Zürich 1937

Das Bürgerhaus der Renaissance in Niederdonau, Richard Kurt Donin, Verlag Karl Kühne, Wien, Leipzig 1944

Kulturgeschichte des Wohnens, Edmund Meier-Oberist, Ferd. Holzmann Verlag, Hamburg 1956

Frühformen der Hausentwicklung in Deutschland, Werner Radig, Dt. Bauakademie, Henschel Verlag, Berlin 1958

Der Wohngarten, Guido Harbers, Callwey Verlag, München 1933

Kayseri Evlery, Necibe Cakirouglu, Istanbul 1952

Wohnung und Siedlung, Paul Wolf, Wasmuth Verlag, Berlin 1926

Vorträge und Aufsätze, Martin Heidegger, Neske Verlag, Pfuhlingen 1954

Der Beginn der Architektur, Siegfried Giedon, Verlag Fretz und Wasmuth, Zürich 1965

Lidova Architektura, Vaclav Mencl, Academia Nakladatelsti, Praha 1980

Das Hofhaus ist tot – es lebe das Hofhaus

Durch das in den letzten Jahrzehnten nie dagewesene Bauvolumen ist die menschlich überschaubare Dimension einer beispielhaften Architektur weitgehend verloren gegangen. Das sprunghafte Anwachsen von brennenden Umweltfragen hat eine Verunsicherung in der Planung hervorgerufen. Unser Interesse konzentriert sich wieder auf das Ursprüngliche, Elementare und Simple. ‹Sparsamkeit ist eine Form der Weisheit›, sagte Lucius Burckhardt. Das einfache räumliche Wohnen und Bauen wird wieder mehr beachtet. Wie war es damals möglich, mit so wenig Komfort die Tradition der Architektur mit dem Lebensprozess zu vereinen und über Jahrhunderte in abgelegenen Gebieten bis heute zu erhalten? Vielleicht könnte uns hier die kühne Behauptung vom ‹Gegenwärtigsein des Vergangenen› wieder zu einstigen Methoden zurückführen, die wir mit den heutigen Mitteln neu interpretieren müssten. Diese dringende Notwendigkeit – also die Abkehr von einem geistlosen Komfort – könnte uns den Weg zur Entstehung einer neuen Tradition von Wohnen und Leben und somit gerade in die Innenhöfe weisen. Die ursprüngliche, elementare Hofhaus-Architektur könnte sich mit dem Lebensprozess vereinen. Die Privatheit des Wohnens braucht eine geschützte Öffnung, ‹sie verlangt eine gegen Störung und Einblick abgeschirmte Erschliessung des Innen und Aussen›, sagt Wend Fischer treffend. Es geht also um das Wesen und die Geschichte einer umlaufenden oder durchbrochenen Wand, die einen Innenhof unter freiem Himmel bildet. Die Interpretation dieses Lichthofes finden wir in wirklichkeitsnahen Hofhausbauten mit der gegliederten geborgenen Mitte bis in phantasievollen Gartenanlagen, in denen die Höfe allein durch die Vegetation bestimmt werden. ‹Die Wand›, so schrieb schon anfangs dieses Jahrhunderts der Architekt und Pädagoge Gottfried Semper in seinem Werk ‹Der Stil›, ‹ist dasjenige bauliche Element, das den eingeschlossenen Raum als solchen gleichsam absolut und ohne Hinweis auf Seitenbegriffe formalität vergegenwärtigt und äusserlich dem Auge kenntlich macht.› Das Wort Wand erinnert an den Ursprung und den Typus des sichtbaren Raumabschlusses. Die Wand umschliesst und begrenzt den Lichthof. Die aktuelle Problemstellung der elementaren Hofhaus-Architektur und ihre Bedeutung soll den Betrachter mit der Frage nach der Weisheit unserer Vorfahren konfrontieren, ohne dass er dabei seine wesentlichen Eigenschaften aufgeben soll. Aus dem Zwang regionaler Bedingungen, von äusseren Einflüssen unberührt, im Bauprozess organisch gewachsen und in die Dynamik landschaftlicher Formen gebaut, scheinen die Bauwerke der elementaren Hofhaus-Architektur mit dem Boden verwachsen zu sein. Die Landschaft wird zum Schutzwall des Bauwerks. In der Anpassung des Massstabs an seine Umgebung wird die Qualität des Baus sichtbar. In der Funktion des abgeschirmten Innenhofes wird der Himmel in das Wohnen miteinbezogen; Prinzipien in der Architektur sind einmalig, man identifiziert sich mit ihnen. Am Beispiel einer Grundlagenarbeit (Illinois Institute of Technology, Chicago) und einer Semesterarbeit an der Hochschule für Angewandte Kunst in Wien (Meisterklasse für Innenarchitektur) sowie mit den Photographien, die während meiner jahrelangen Suche nach Höfen in der Architektur entstanden sind, soll der Versuch gemacht werden, aus der Denkweise der Hofhausidee in der Vergangenheit, Anregungen für die Diskussion der Probleme der Gegenwart zu schöpfen. Das Hofhaus ist tot – es lebe das Hofhaus.

The courtyard house is dead – long live the courtyard house!

Architecture on a human scale that might serve as an example has been largely lost to view in the unprecedented volume of building done during recent decades. Environmental problems have cropped up left, right and centre, and no planner can be sure of his bearings. Our interest has been refocused on the original, elementary and simple. Economy is a form of wisdom, said Lucius Burckhardt. Living that is simple, undemanding in space, unpretentious in structure, is regaining respect. How was it possible in bygone days, when amenities were so modest, to unite architectural tradition and the living process and, in remote places, to maintain the tradition down to the present? The 'presence of the past' is a bold notion but perhaps it can help us to return to the methods of former days and reinterpret them with the resources of today. This fundamental necessity – the renunciation of a vacuous comfort – would point the way to a new tradition of homes and living, and nowhere more strikingly than in the inner courtyard. Thus the original architecture of the courtyard house could become part and parcel of our living process.

The privacy of the home calls for a protected entrance: 'there must be access from the interior to the exterior through an opening screened against distur-

bances and prying eyes', as Wend Fischer put it very aptly. What is involved, then, is the function and history of a wall, continuous or interrupted, which encloses an inner courtyard under the open sky. This courtyard can be interpreted in many ways ranging from sober courtyard houses integrated with the patterned hortus seclusus to highly imaginative gardens where the vegetation dictates how the courts should be. The point was neatly made by the architect and educationist Gottfried Semper in his book 'Style' at the beginning of this century: 'The wall is the structural element which formally identifies the enclosed space in absolute terms, as it were, and without reference to trivialities and marks it as such externally to the eye.' The word wall recalls the origin and type of the visible spatial enclosure. The wall encloses and delimits our courtyard. The problems currently raised by the courtyard house and its importance for us bring home to the observer the wisdom of our forefathers without at the same time compromising any of the essential characteristics of this architecture.

Unaffected by extraneous influences, serving the needs created by regional conditions, buildings like elementary courtyard houses, which have grown in a structural organic process and con-

form to the dynamics of the landscape, seem to be part of the earth they stand on. The landscape becomes a bastion protecting the structure. By the adaptation of its scale to the environment, the quality of the building is manifested. Screened off from outside, the inner court has the function of bringing the sky into the home; such principles in architecture are unique and identification with them is salutary.

With a grounding at the Illinois Institute of Technology for basic reference and a six-month term in the master class for interior decoration at the College of Applied Arts in Vienna, I, armed with my camera, have been engaged for many years in a quest for courtyards in architecture. I feel the time has now come to examine the thinking behind the courtyard house of the past in order to elicit ideas that may be fruitful in our discussions of the problems of the present.

The courtyard house is dead – long live the courtyard house!

Atrium als Beispiel

Das abendländische Hofhaus geht in erster Linie auf das antike Atrium zurück. Dieses entwickelte sich aus dem Herdhaus, in dessen Dachmitte sich ein Rauchabzugloch befand, welches sich im Impluvium wiederfindet. Das Atrium, im Verhältnis 5:3 oder 3:2, war der Hof einer solchen Bauweise und ein grösseres mit Säulen umgebenes Peristyl war angeschlossen. Die Belichtung erfolgte ausschliesslich vom Hof her, der aber auch als Verkehrsweg für die Zimmer diente.

Atrium as example

The courtyard house in the West can be traced back primarily to the antique atrium. This developed from the fire-hearth building, in the roof of which there was a hole for the smoke. A similar opening was found above the impluvium. The atrium with sides in the ratio of 5:3 or 3:2 formed the courtyard of such a building, and connected to it was a larger peristyle surrounded by columns. Light was obtained solely from the courtyard, which also served as a traffic route to the rooms.

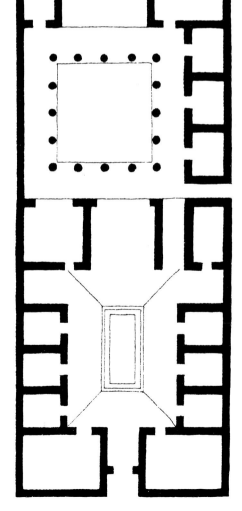

Grundriss eines römischen Hauses mit Peristyl.

Plan of a Roman house with peristyle.

Vettier-Atrium-Haus, Pompeji, 1. Jahrhundert n. Chr.

In den Kulturen des Südens war der
innere, offene Raum verschiedenartig
konzipiert: vom kleinen Hof oder dem
ringsum vom überstehenden Dach teilweise überdeckten Innenhof bis zu den
Säulenhöfen der Ägypter und Griechen,
die dann bei den Römern in dem uns
bekannten Pompejianer Atrium-Haus
ihre Fortführung fanden. Innerhalb eines
rechteckigen Volumens sind Räume
symmetrisch angeordnet. Der Mittelraum, das Atrium, bekommt Licht durch
die Deckenöffnung. Das darunter aufge-
stellte Becken, das Impluvium, sammelt
das Regenwasser. In der Achse des
Eingangs liegt der Speiseraum, das
Tablinum. Von dort kommt man in den
Garten, der vielfach nach griechischem
Vorbild von Säulenhallen umgeben ist,
dem Peristyl.

Vettier atrium house, Pompeii,
1st cent. AD

In the civilizations of southern countries
this open court in the centre of the
building took a variety of forms: it
might be a small courtyard, or one
partly covered by the projecting roof, or
the colonnaded court of the Egyptians
and Greeks, which was then continued
as the atrium house familiar to us from
Pompeii. The rooms are symmetrically
arranged inside a rectangular block. The
central space, the atrium, receives light
through an opening in the roof. The tank
placed under the opening, the impluvium, collects the rainwater. The dining
room, the tablinum, lies on the
entrance axis. From there one proceeds
into the garden, which is often surrounded by colonnades in the Greek
style, thus forming the peristyle.

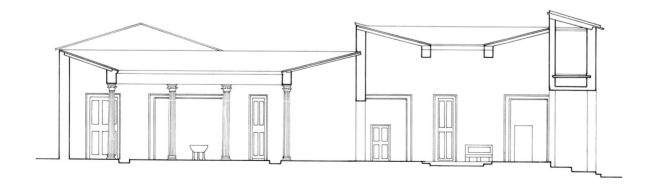

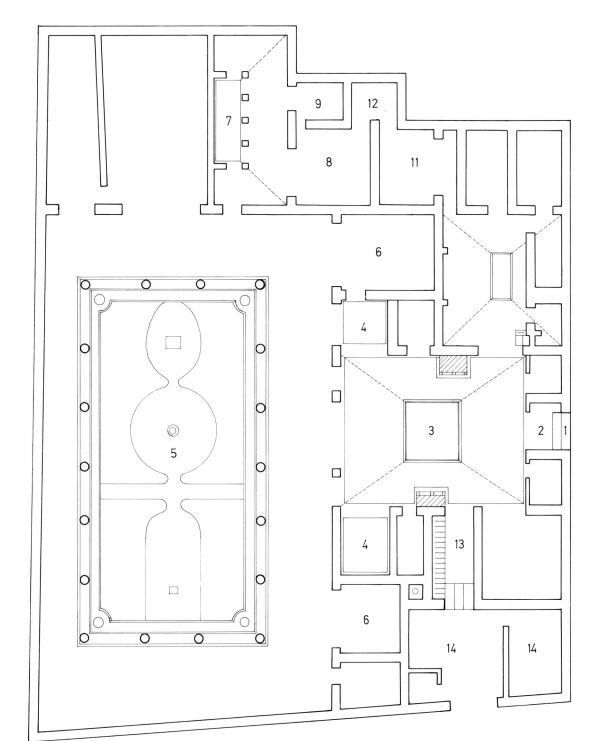

1 Vestibulum
2 Fauces
3 Atrium
4 Alae
5 Peristyl
  Peristyle
6 Speisezimmer
  Dining room
7 Kleines Peristyl
  Small peristyle
8 Speisezimmer
  Dining room
9 Schlafzimmer
  Bedroom
10 Nebenatrium
  Side atrium
11 Küche
  Kitchen
12 Kammer
  Storeroom
13 Korridor
  Corridor
14 Nebenräume
  Subsidiary rooms

Haus der Vettier in Pompeji, Massstab
1:200.

House of the Vettier in Pompeii, scale
1:200.

Das arabische Hofhaus

Im arabischen Kulturbereich unterscheiden wir folgende Hofhaustypen: Den nur mit Mauern erzeugten freien Hofraum im Haus oder den Hofraum, der sich aus Gebäudeteilen (z.B. Festung) bildet. Höfe erweitern sich durch Arkaden oder werden auch durch Galerien gebildet. Diese Häuser machen einen leicht transparenten, luftigen Eindruck, obwohl sie nach aussen geschlossen sind. Der Hof mit Arkadengängen und Kuppelgewölben ist die erste Versammlungsstätte der Gläubigen. Regelmässige, geometrische Grundformen und glatte ornamentlose Wände sind die baukünstlerischen Merkmale. Ein beispielhaftes Bauwerk dieser Art finden wir in der Alhambra (Granada, Andalusien). Noch heute ist diese Wohnform mit einem Lichthof über weite Teile im islamischen Bereich, wenn auch stark verändert, erhalten geblieben. Die heutigen Bewohner erkennen im Hofhaus eine Möglichkeit für vielfältiges Leben im Dienste einer verbesserten Wohnqualität. Im Zentrum dieser Wohnform stehen die nach der Freifläche geöffneten Gebäude oder die umlaufende Mauer, die den Hof bilden, sodass der Wohnhof den Eindruck eines Zimmers ohne Dach macht. Die Weite des Himmels ist in den Wohnhof miteinbezogen.

Oasenstadt El Qued in Algerien

Die Oasensiedlung ist für die einheimische Bevölkerung ein interessantes, funktionsfähiges, zweckmässiges und sehr vielseitiges ‹Habitat›, realisiert mit der einfachsten zur Verfügung stehenden Materie: Lehm. Aus der Vogelperspektive gesehen, bilden die organisierten, aneinandergereihten Kuppeldächer – in ortsüblicher Lehmbauweise mit einem durchschnittlichen Durchmesser von ca. 225 cm konstruiert – mit den dazugehörenden intimen Wohnhofräumen ein geordnetes, zusammenhängendes Ganzes.

Arabian courtyard house

In Arabian countries the following types of courtyard house are found: an open court in the house created by walls alone, or courtyards which are formed out of parts of buildings, e.g. a fortress. The size of the courts is increased by arcades or the latter are formed by galleries. The most fully developed form is the courtyard created by arcades and galleries. The impression evoked by these houses is one of lightness and transparency, even though they are closed to the outside. In the mosque the court surrounded by arcaded walks with domical vaults is the first meeting-place of the faithful. The architectural features are basic forms of regular geometrical shape and smooth walls devoid of ornament. An exemplary work of this kind is to be found in the Alhambra (Granada, Andalusia). Even today this type of house with an inner court is found in many parts of the Islamic world, though it has been greatly modified. The present-day inhabitants see in the courtyard house a means of enhancing the quality of life in a diversified pattern. The heart and centre of this house is formed by the buildings facing onto the open space or the enclosing walls which form the court. The impression created is of a room without a roof.

The oasis town of El Qued in Algeria

Oasis settlements are built from the simplest material available – clay – and are interesting in the way in which they provide a functionally efficient habitat for the people living there. The dome roofs, constructed from clay in the traditional way and measuring some 225 cm across, are seen from above to be arranged in rows and, along with the intimate inner courts, make up an ordered and coherent pattern.

Oasenstadt El Qued in Algerien, Massstab 1:500.

Oasis town of El Qued in Algeria, scale 1:500.

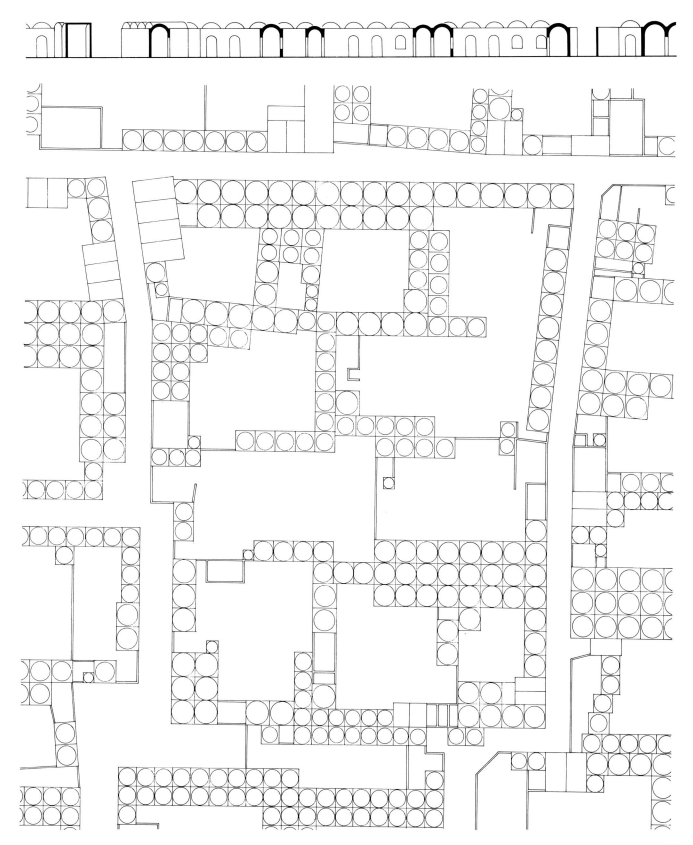

Kulthöfe in der Türkei

Der Vorhof der Moschee mit umschliessenden Arkadengängen in Gewölbekuppeln ist die erste Versammlungsstätte der Gläubigen. Die kleineren Gewölbekammern, ein archaisches Prinzip in halbzylindrischer Form, bilden die Grundzelle. Die horizontal betonten Arkaden schaffen eine angenehme Verbindung zwischen Innen- und Aussenraum. Die Abgrenzung von offenem zu gedecktem Raum geht dadurch nahtlos ineinander über. Ein weiteres typisches Merkmal im Vorhof ist das oft in der Achse liegende Wasserbecken. Wasser gilt als lebenserhaltende Kostbarkeit; es bringt Kühlung und Erfrischung. Wie wichtig die Orient-Architektur für uns sein kann, zeigen die um 1911 entstandenen Skizzenbücher des Charles-Edouard Jeanneret (Le Corbusier) mit seinen architektonischen Skizzen von Moscheen aus Istanbul. Während seiner grossen Reisen entdeckte Le Corbusier hinter dem Reichtum des Dekors auch die bestimmenden räumlichen Verhältnisse. In seinem Werk ‹Vers une architecture› wurde die Moschee als Beispiel eines Bauens von innen nach aussen und einer nach dem Prinzip der Steigerung aufgebauten Raumfolge interpretiert, schrieb Wolfgang Pehnt in seinem Aufsatz ‹Der Orient und die Architektur des 19. und 20. Jahrhunderts› (Ausstellungskatalog Weltkultur und moderne Kunst, München 1972). Drei wesentliche Elemente der klassischen islamischen Architektur zeigen, dass sie auch für uns Gültigkeit haben. Erstens: additives Element (serielle Gliederung), zweitens: struktives Element (konstruktives Gefüge), drittens: texturales Element (dekorative Gestalt).

Mosque courtyards in Turkey

The forecourt of the mosque is surrounded by arcades of domical vaults and represents the first meeting-place of the faithful. The smaller vaulted chambers, an archaic principle in semicylindrical form, constitute the additive units. The horizontal accentuation of the arcades creates a pleasing link between interior and exterior and ensures that covered and open spaces form an unbroken continuum. Another typical element of the forecourt is the pool, which often lies on the axis, affording coolth and refreshment, and makes a precious, life-sustaining feature. How important oriental architecture may be for us is underlined in the sketchbooks made in 1911 by Charles-Edouard Jeanneret (Le Corbusier) with their architectural surveys of mosques in Istanbul. On his travels Le Corbusier discovered behind the surface ornamentation the spatial structure. In Le Corbusier's work 'Vers une architecture' the mosque is quoted as an example of a building created from inwards outwards, with space added to space on a principle of crescendo, wrote Wolfgang Pehnt in his essay 'Der Orient und die Architektur des 19. und 20. Jh.' (Exhibition catalogue 'Weltkultur und moderne Kunst', Munich 1972). Three elements essential to classical Islamic architecture show that its principles also hold good for us. First: the additive element (serial articulation), second: the structural element (constructive composition), third: the textural element (form as decoration).

39
Haus von Murad II in Bursa, 18. Jh.

House of Murad II in Bursa, 18th cent.

Skizze von Le Corbusier aus den
‹Carnets de voyage›, 1911, Bauernhaus
in Muratli.

Sketch by Le Corbusier from the
'Carnets de voyage', 1911. Farmhouse
in Muratli.

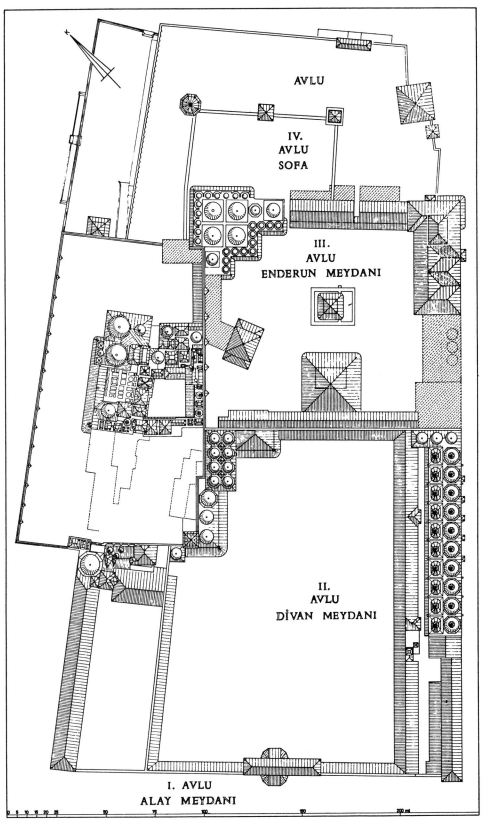

AVLU

IV.
AVLU
SOFA

III.
AVLU
ENDERUN MEYDANI

II.
AVLU
DİVAN MEYDANI

Top-Kapi Sarayi, Istanbul, 15.–18. Jh.

Top-Kapi Sarayi, Istanbul, 15th–18th cent.

I. AVLU
ALAY MEYDANI

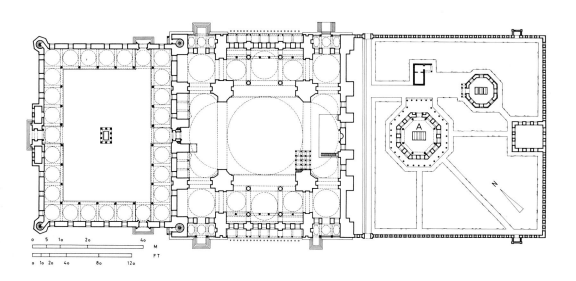

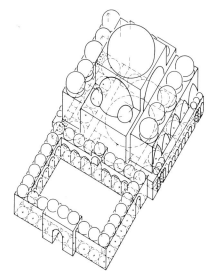

Suleymaniye-Moschee in Istanbul,
1550–1556.
Die Kugeln und Zylinder der Moscheen
sind dieselben geometrischen Formen,
die Le Corbusier als Grundlage seiner
Ästhetik proklamierte.

Suleymaniye mosque in Istanbul,
1550–1556.
The sphere and cylinder of the
mosques are the same geometric
forms as Le Corbusier proclaimed to be
the basis of his aesthetics.

43
Fatich-Moschee in Istanbul: Die
Moschee ist ein ‹civic center›.

Fatih mosque in Istanbul; the courtyard
of the mosque is a 'civic centre'.

Top-Kapi-Sarayi, Arkaden umschliessen
die Höfe.

Top-Kapi Sarayi, arcades enclose the
courtyard.

44

Alhambra (arabisch al hamra = die Rote),
Burg über Granada,
13.–14. Jahrhundert.

Mit der Alhambra (Andalusien) in Granada ist eine kostbare arabische Hofanlage bewahrt: kanalartige Bassins, Springbrunnen und von Arkaden umgebene Höfe. Das dazugehörige Lustschloss ‹Generalife› aus der zweiten Hälfte des 18. Jahrhunderts liegt auf dem Alhambrahügel im arabischen Stil gebaut: Zypressengärten und Wasserspiele mit Fontänen umrahmen kühle Patios. Die Alhambra zeigt eine aussergewöhnliche, interessante Entwicklung des Gartenhofhauses im arabischen Kulturbereich. Die Höfe machen einen leicht transparenten, luftigen Eindruck, obwohl sie nach aussen fast vollständig geschlossen sind.
Im Löwenhof, in dem 12 Marmorlöwen das grosse Wasserbecken tragen, bedecken Fayencen und ziselierte Stuckplatten die Wände. Eine Symbiose zwischen Orient und Okzident finden wir im zweigeschossigen Säulenhof des Renaissancepalastes von Karl V.: Klassische Säulen mit ionischen Kapitellen zieren die Wandelhalle im Obergeschoss; im Erdgeschoss bilden Säulen mit dorischen Kapitellen den Abschluss des runden Hofraumes. Das Gebäude wurde von Pedro Machuca gebaut und besteht aus zwei Elementen: dem quadratischen Grundriss und einem kreisförmigen Innenhof.

Alhambra (Arab. al hamra = the red one)
castle above Granada,
13th–14th centuries.

The Alhambra in Granada preserves for us a precious example of an Arabian courtyard complex: water basins, fountains and courts surrounded by arcades. The villa 'Generalife', also part of the complex, is situated on the Alhambra hill. It was built in Arabian style and dates from the second half of the 18th century. Cool courtyards are surrounded by cypress woods and there are fountains and water displays. The Alhambra records an extraordinarily interesting development of the garden courtyard house in Arabian civilization. The courtyards make a light and airy impression even though they are almost completely shut off from outside.
Light and water play a prominent role in Islamic architecture. The mirroring surface of the pool and the slabs of stone capture the light, reflect it into the buildings, and transmute everything into a transcendental world. Water is the source of freshness and the symbol of purity. This subtle interplay of water and light is particularly prominent in the Alhambra Palace (14th cent. AD) in Granada. In the Court of the Lions, where 12 marble lions support the great water basin, the walls are covered with faience and carved stuccowork. In the Renaissance palace of Charles V there is a symbiosis of East and West: classical columns with Ionic capitals contrast with rows of pillars topped by cubic capitals. The Pedro Machuca building is notable for two elements: a square plan and a circular inner court.

46–67
Die Alhambra in Granada, 13.–14. Jh., ein Meisterwerk der maurischen Kunst.

Alhambra in Granada, 13th–14th cent.
A masterpiece of Moorish art.

PLANO GENERAL DE LA ALHAMBRA Y EL GENERALIFE

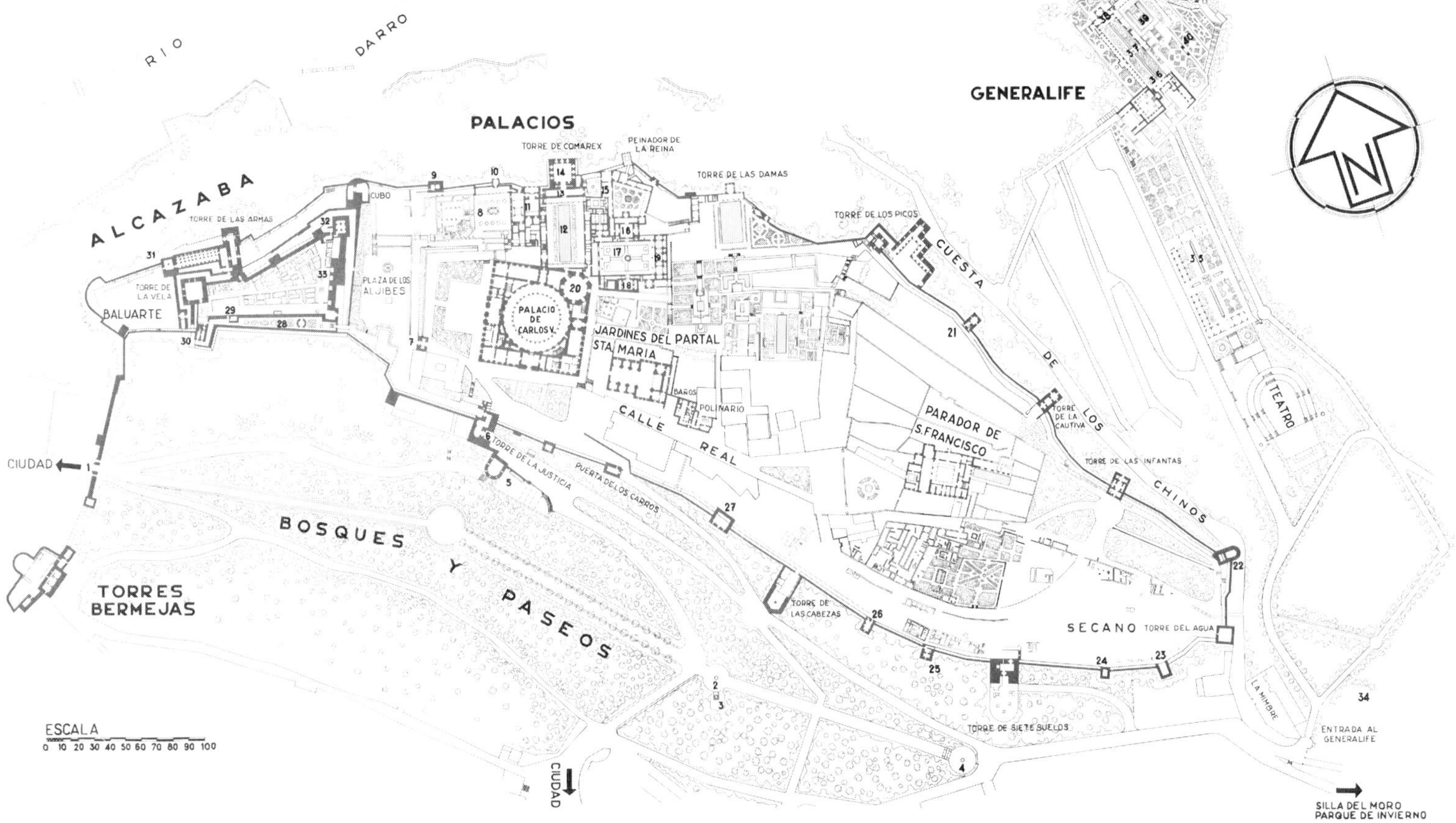

RIO   DARRO

GENERALIFE

PALACIOS

TORRE DE COMAREX   PEINADOR DE LA REINA

TORRE DE LAS DAMAS

ALCAZABA

9   10   14

CUBO   8   11

TORRE DE LAS ARMAS   32   12   16

31   35   17

TORRE DE LA VELA   PLAZA DE LOS ALJIBES   18

BALUARTE   29   20

30   28 ( )   PALACIO DE CARLOS V.

7

JARDINES DEL PARTAL

STA MARIA

TORRE DE LOS PICOS

CUESTA

21

TEATRO   bajo

DE   LOS

TORRE DE LA CAUTIVA

PARADOR DE S. FRANCISCO

CALLE   REAL

BAÑOS   POLINARIO

CIUDAD ← 1

6 TORRE DE LA JUSTICIA

5   PUERTA DE LOS CARROS

TORRE DE LAS INFANTAS

CHINOS

BOSQUES   27

22

TORRES BERMEJAS

Y   TORRE DE LAS CABEZAS   26

PASEOS   25   SECANO   TORRE DEL AGUA

24   23

LA MIMBRE   34

CIUDAD ↓

2   TORRE DE SIETE SUELOS

3

4   ENTRADA AL GENERALIFE

ESCALA
0 10 20 30 40 50 60 70 80 90 100

SILLA DEL MORO →
PARQUE DE INVIERNO

N

47

48–49
Palacio de Carlos V, Innenhof. Symbiose zwischen Orient- und Occident im Renaissancepalast Karls V. nach Plänen des Italieners Pedro Machuca gebaut.

Palacio de Carlos V, inner court. Symbiosis of Eastern and Western elements in the Renaissance palace of Charles V, built to plans of the Italian Pedro Machuca.

50–51
Patio del Mexuar (Mexuarhof), Wände
mit islamischer Flächendekoration.

Patio del Mexuar (Mexuar Court), walls
with Islamic surface decoration.

52–54
Patio de los Arrayanes (Myrtenhof).

Patio de los Arrayanes (Court of the Myrtles).

Licht und Wasser spielen eine wichtige Rolle. Steinplatten reflektieren das Licht.

Light and ornamental waterworks figure prominently. Stone slabs reflect the light.

54
Myrtenhof, Wasser als Quelle der Frische und als Symbol der Reinheit. Ein kanalartiges Bassin durchschneidet fast die ganze Länge des von Arkaden umgebenen Hofes.

Court of the Myrtles; water as a source of coolth and a symbol of purity. A channel-like basin runs almost the whole length of the court, which is surrounded by arcades.

55
Patio de la Reja (Hof mit vier alten Zypressen).

Patio de la Reja (court with four old cypresses).

56–59
Patio de los Leones (Löwenhof).

Patio de los Leones (Court of the Lions).

Zwölf Marmorlöwen tragen das grosse Wasserbecken.

Twelve marble lions bear the large water basin.

58–59
Löwenhof, seine Arkaden, Säulen und Stucke dienten weltweit als Modelle für Ausstellungspavillons im 19. Jh.

The Court of the Lions, its arcades, its pillars and stuccos were taken as models for exhibition pavilions all over the world in the 19th century.

60–67
El Generalife, das maurische Garten-
schloss etwa aus dem 18. Jh. Wasser
und Vegetation, zwei Elemente des
Lustgartens.

El Generalife, the Moorish villa dating
from the 18th cent. Water and planting
are two elements of the pleasure
garden.

Patio architektonisch gebildet mit Kie-
selsteinpflasterung.

The patio is given an architectural pattern by the pebble paving.

62–63
Patio del Cipres de la Sultana (Hof der Zypressen der Sultanin).
Wandelgänge mit beschnittenen Zypressen und gemustertem Kieselsteinpflaster führen zu den Gärten des Theaters.

Patio del Cipres de la Sultana (Court of the Sultana's Cypresses).
Covered walks with trimmed cypresses and patterned paving leading to the Gardens of the Theatre.

64–65
Patio de la Acaquia, Hof der Springbrunnen mit Bewässerungskanal.

Patio de la Acaquia (Court of the Fountains), court with irrigation channel.

66
Phantasien mit intimen Winkeln durch
Zypressen realisiert.

Intimate corners created imaginatively
with cypresses.

67
Convento de la Francisco, ehemaliges
Franziskanerkloster auf der Alhambra
1332–54, heute als Parador (Touri-
stenhotel) mit z.T. arabischer Konstruktion.

Convento de la Francisco, former Fran-
ciscan monastery on the Alhambra,
1332–54. Today a Parador tourist
hotel of partly Arabian construction.

Hofhäuser des Iran

Im Unterschied zu den Hofhäusern der griechischen und römischen Antike, die sich um mehrere Höfe gruppieren, zeichnet sich das Hofhaus des Irans durch einen einzigen grossen Hof aus. Die Räume und Hallen der Gebäude um diesen Hof hat man mit Ziegelgewölben überdeckt und damit viele Aufgaben gleichzeitig erfüllt: wie Tragfähigkeit, Wärmedämmung, Akustik. Die einzigen Baustoffe solcher Häuser sind Lehm, Sand, Kalk und ein wenig Holz.

Courtyard houses in Iran

In contrast to the courtyard houses of Greek and Roman antiquity, which are grouped round a number of courts, the courtyard house of Iran has but one large court. The rooms and halls in the buildings round this court are covered by brick vaults which simultaneously serve the purposes of load-bearing, heat insulation and acoustics. These houses are built of clay, sand, lime and a little wood.

1 Wohnraum
  Living room
2 Schlafraum
  Bedroom
3 Küche
  Kitchen
4 Abstellraum
  Storeroom
5 Toilette
  Toilet
6 Winterwohnraum
  Winter living room
7 Gästezimmer
  Guestroom
8 Hof
  Courtyard
9 Essplatz
  Dining area
10 Eingang
   Entrance
11 Gartenausgang
   Garden exit
12 Wasserbecken
   Water basin
13 Strasse
   Street
14 Belüftungsöffnung
   Ventilation opening

Zweifamilienhaus in Bafg-Iran, Massstab 1:200.

Two-family house in Bafg, Iran, scale 1:200.

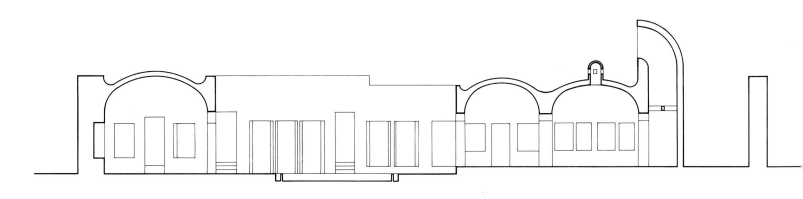

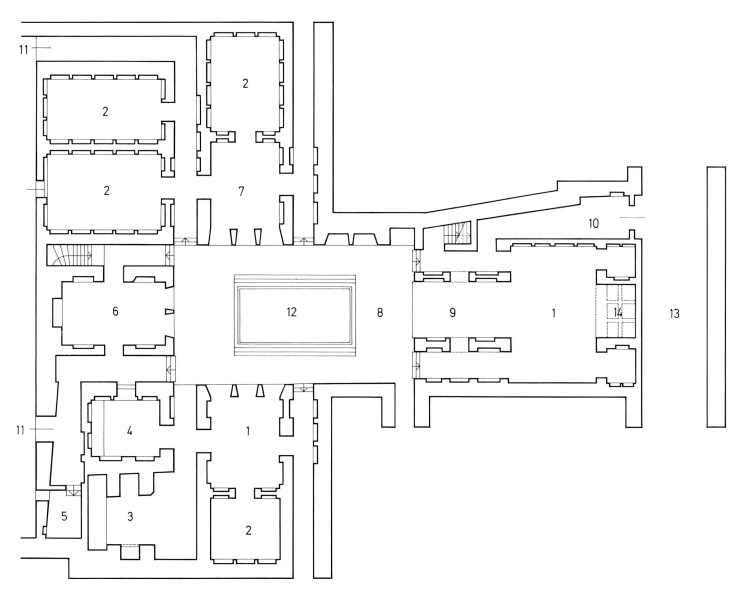

Fernöstliche Hofhaustypen

Gerade in unserer Zeit wird der Wunsch nach dem Lichtspender eines Atriums als individuelle Freiheit angesehen. In der Volksrepublik China geht der aus dem 19. Jahrhundert stammende Hofhaustyp, der heute noch benützt wird, auf die Han-Zeit (3. Jahrhundert vor bis 3. Jahrhundert n. Chr.) zurück. Dieser Wohntyp mit vier Gebäuden um einen quadratischen Hof ist die älteste Form des Hofhauses. Er lässt sich auch bei Tempeln und Palästen finden. Der an seinen vier Seiten umschlossene Hof wird als das Sinnbild eines quadratischen Raumes, einer vollkommenen und unabhängigen Welt verstanden. Bei grösseren Gebäudeanlagen lässt sich das Grundschema des quadratischen Hofes multiplizieren, ohne der Beständigkeit des Urtyps zu schaden.

In der klassischen Architektur Japans bilden Garten und Innenraum zusammen den vorbildlichen Wohnraum. Die Schiebetüren, die Aussen und Innen voneinander trennen, sind in ihrer Wirkung wie Vorhänge von stärkster Stabilität. Der Innenraum und der begrenzte Aussenraum sind in erster Linie Orte der Besinnung, und der Meditation. Darum ist der Raum leer und beseelt zugleich. Er ist ein Teil der beseelten Natur, des Universums mit dem der Meditierende sich in Harmonie vereinigt.

Chinesisches Hofhaus

Typisch für die chinesischen Hofhäuser in Beijing, den sogenannten Hu'-t'ungs (kleinen Alleehäusern), ist die Ausrichtung entlang einer Hauptachse; mit Vorliebe in Nord-Süd-Richtung, sonst das Prinzip des Rechteckes und der Parallelität. Jedes grössere Ensemble von Bauwerken und Räumen wird von einer Wand umgeben, sei es nun ein kaiserlicher Palast oder eine einfache Dorfanlage. Die Einfassung der Baugruppe mit einer festen Mauer entspricht der scharfen Grenze, die zwischen der eigenen Familie und der Umwelt gezogen

wird. Bedeutungsvoll bleibt Beijing's Stadtbild in seiner imperialen Grösse früherer Dynastien und der sorgfältigen Konservierung der historischen Bau- und Kunstwerke. Die grossen Parks mit Pavillons, Wandelgalerien und Märchenlandschaften, in denen sich einst Prinzen und ihre Kurtisanen vergnügt haben, sind im früheren Glanz dem gesamten Volk zugänglich.

Eine weit verbreitete Bauart von Wohnbauten grossen und kleineren Massstabs in Beijing war seit jeher der vierseitig umschlossene Hof. Er war die typische Wohneinheit der oberen Schichten der feudalistischen Zeit. Regelmässigkeit in der Anordnung und Gleichförmigkeit des Stils waren charakteristische Elemente dieser Anlagen. Der Siedlungstyp ist über weites Terrain in eine grössere Zahl von mit Mauern umgebenen Höfen eingeteilt. Der Hof als Lichtspender ist von Gebäuden umgeben, an die, entlang der Mittelachse, weitere Höfe gereiht sind. Die Hauptgebäude waren aus kosmologischen Gründen meistens nach Süden gerichtet. Der Weg vom Eingang bis zur hintersten Haupthalle war ‹der Weg nach oben›.

Far Eastern types of courtyard house

Today especially the atrium as a source of light is conceived in terms of individual freedom. In the People's Republic of China the type of courtyard house which has been preserved from the 19th century and is still used today goes right back to the Han dynasty (3rd cent. BC to 3rd cent. AD). This type, in which four buildings are grouped round a square court, is the oldest form of courtyard house. It can also be used in temples and palaces. The courtyard surrounded by its four walls is seen as an image of an independent world of perfection, symbolized by the square. In large complexes the basic plan of the square court can be multiplied without affecting the unbroken harmony of the original type.

In the classical architecture of Japan the garden and interior room together constitute a living area of exemplary quality. The sliding doors which separate inside from outside are like solid curtains. The interior and the limited exterior are primarily a place of meditation. That is why the room is empty and yet pervaded by spirit. It is part of the spirit of nature, the universe, with which the meditator seeks to unite himself.

Chinese courtyard house

Typical features of the Chinese courtyard houses in Beijing, the Hu'-t'ungs as they are called (small alley houses), are the disposition along a main axis, preferably in a north-south direction, and the principle of rectangularity and parallelism. Every major complex of buildings and spaces, whether an imperial palace or a simple village layout, is surrounded by an enclosing wall. This enclosure of the group of buildings by a strong wall is a reflection of the sharp dividing line drawn between the family and the environment. The townscape of

Beijing has been preserved in the imperial grandeur of earlier dynasties and is resplendent with historical works of art and architecture. The great parks, where once princes and courtesans disported themselves in pavilions and covered walks and amidst fairy landscapes, have been made generally accessible in all their former glory. The enclosed inner court of four sides has always been a commonly adopted form of structure for dwelling houses, large and small, in Beijing. It was the typical home of the upper classes during the feudalistic period. Regularity of arrangement and uniformity of style were characteristic elements of these layouts. The pattern of settlement over a wide area embraces a large number of cells comprising courtyards surrounded by walls. As a source of light the court is surrounded by buildings to which other buildings can be added in a row along the central axis. For cosmological reasons the main building was usually constructed facing south. The path from the entrance to the rearmost main hall was the path upwards.

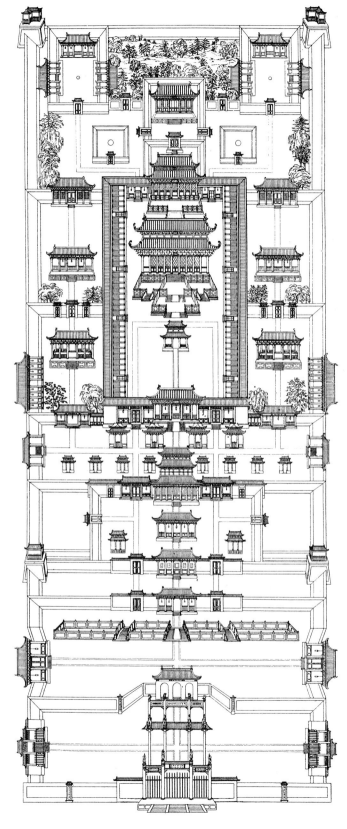

71–87
Chinesische Hofhaus-Architektur.

Chinese courtyard house architecture.

Rollbild: Legende von der Entführung
der Fürstin Wen-chi

In den uns wohlbekannten alten chinesischen Holzschnitten sind vielfach die
Landschaftsbilder mit ihren einkompo-
nierten Pavillons aus der Vogelperspektive dargestellt. In diesen Darstellungen
haben die Pavillons zeltartigen Charakter. Eine Legende ‹Wen-chi› aus der
Zeit vor Christus, die in einem Rollbild
aus der Sung-Dynastie (960–1272)
überliefert ist, zeigt Mongolenjurten mit
zusammenlegbaren Wohnzelten und
Szenen, wie eine Prinzessin von den
Barbaren in die Mongolei entführt wird.
Unterwegs lässt die Prinzessin Zeltlager
aufschlagen: mannshohe Stellwände
aus blauem Tuch werden mit Seilen
verspannt und vor dem eigentlichen Zelt
aufgestellt, das sie wie ein Zaun (Sicht-
schutz) abschirmen. Diese Kombina-
tion der Zeltarchitektur und Zeltumzäu-
nung in der freien Natur, die jeden
Abend neu errichtet wird, ist mit
unglaublicher Schönheit in Farbe und
mit grosser Grazilität dargestellt. Hier
wird die mobile Wand innerhalb der
Zeltarchitektur vorbildhaft gezeigt. Wir
lernen, wie symmetrisch angeordnete,
subtil in die Natur gestellte, mobile
Wandelemente in vollendeter Harmonie
mit der Umwelt klar und sauber kompo-
niert wurden.

Scroll painting: legend of the abduction
of Princess Wen-chi

In the Chinese woodcuts, which are so
familiar to us, we often find landscapes
with pavilions seen from above. In
these pictures the pavilions are like
tents. A legend, 'Wen-chi', dating from
the pre-Christian era and handed down
to us in a scroll painting of the Sung
dynasty (960–1272), shows us Mon-
golian yurts, collapsible skin tents, and
the abduction of a princess to Mongolia
by the barbarians. On the journey the
princess has a tented camp set up:
movable walls of blue cloth, as high as a
man, are tautened with ropes and
erected in front of the actual tent,
where they serve as a screen. This com-
bination of tent architecture and tent
enclosure in the open air, erected afresh
every evening, is depicted with
extraordinary felicity of colour and
gracefulness. The movable wall in tent
architecture can still serve as a model
for us today. We see how mobile wall
elements, arranged symmetrically and
subtly integrated with nature, can be
composed so as to harmonize neatly
and clearly with the tent and the environment.

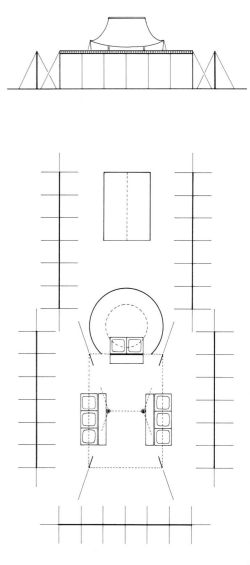

Wen-chi, Wohnzelte (Rekonstruktion)
Massstab 1:200.

Wen-chi, portable tents (reconstruction) scale 1:200.

74–77
Kaiserliche Anlagen mit Höfen in Beijing.

Imperial palaces with courtyards in Beijing.

74
Ku-kung Palastmuseum (früher Verbotene Stadt in Beijing).

Ku-kung palace museum (formerly Forbidden City of Beijing).

75
I-ho-yüan, Sommerpalast, ‹Park der Pflege der Harmonie›, Beijing Dachlandschaft, Ziegel im ‹Mönch- und Nonne›-Verband.

I-ho-yüan, summer palace, the Park of Harmony, Beijing roofscape, over-tile and under-tile roofing.

76–77
Klassisches Hu-t'tung-Alleehofhaus in Beijing, Ching Dynastie (1644–1911), heute Hsi-shih-Allee, Kindergarten, Massstab 1:200.

Classical Hu-t'ung alley courtyard house in Beijing, Ching dynasty (1644–1911), today Hsi-shih Avenue kindergarten, scale 1:200.

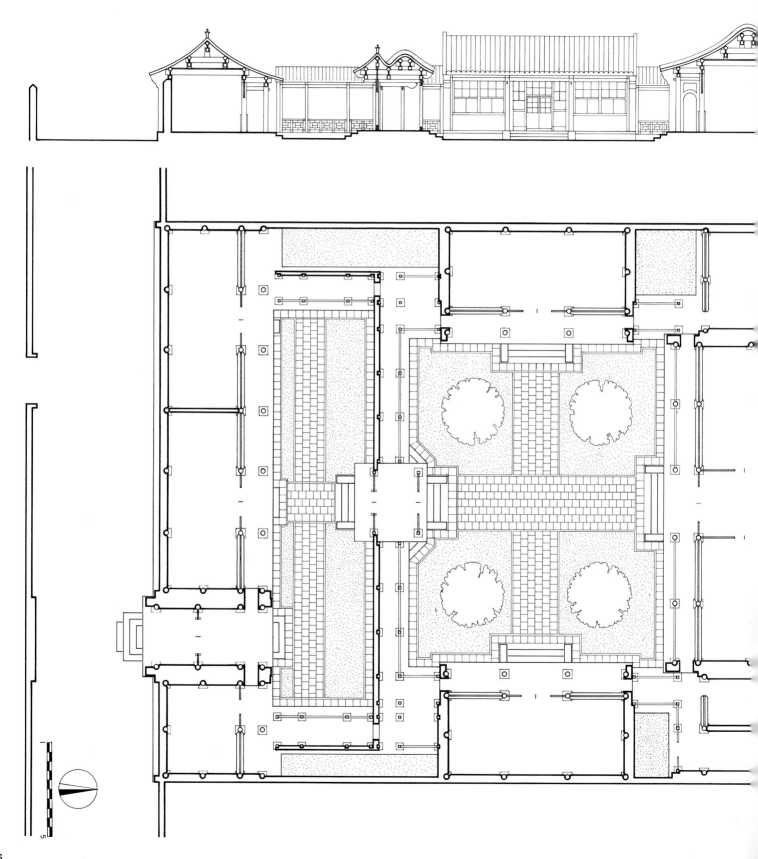

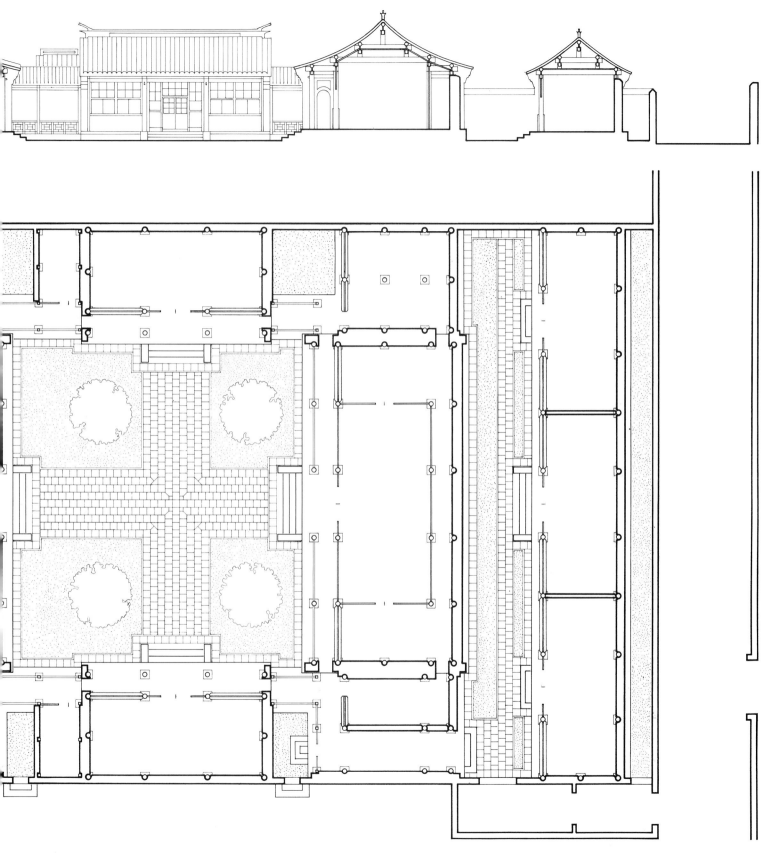

78
Hsiang-shan Park, Hügel des Wohlgeruchs. Der Lichthof wird durch das Wasser des halbrunden Teichs gebildet.

Hsiang-shan Park, Hill of Fragrance. The courtyard is created by the water of the semicircular pool.

79
Mondtore als Zugänge zu den Wohnhofbauten.

Moon gates as entrances to the buildings of the courtyard.

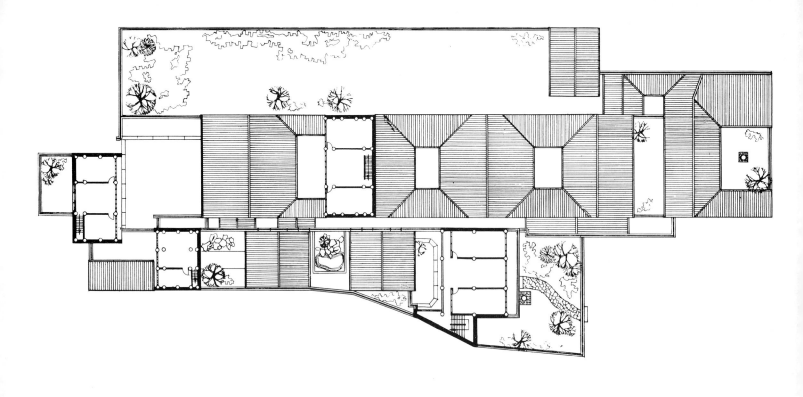

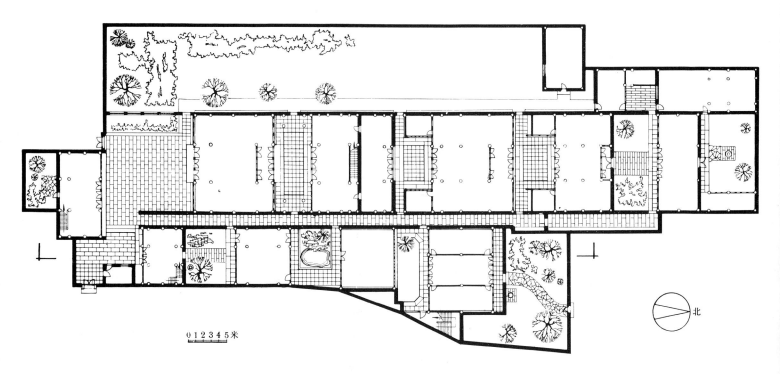

012345米

80–85
Hofhäuser aus Soochow, südlich des
Yang-tze. Grundriss einer Hofhausan-
lage mit Dachaufsicht.

Courtyard houses in Soochow, south of
the Yang-tze. Plan of courtyard houses
with top view.

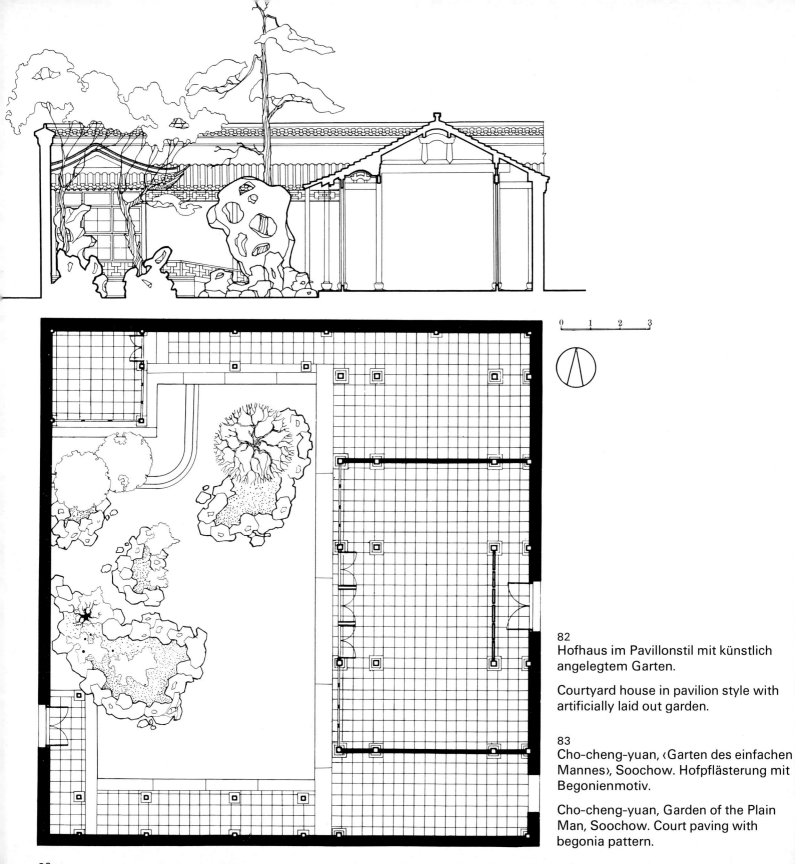

82
Hofhaus im Pavillonstil mit künstlich angelegtem Garten.

Courtyard house in pavilion style with artificially laid out garden.

83
Cho-cheng-yuan, ‹Garten des einfachen Mannes›, Soochow. Hofpflästerung mit Begonienmotiv.

Cho-cheng-yuan, Garden of the Plain Man, Soochow. Court paving with begonia pattern.

84–85
Hsi-yuan-ssu, ‹Der westliche Garten-
tempel›, Soochow, 1635

Hsi-yuan-ssu, Western Garden Temple,
Soochow, 1635.

84
Zugang zum ersten Hof.

Entrance to first courtyard.

85
Galerien im Innenhof.

Galleries in the inner court.

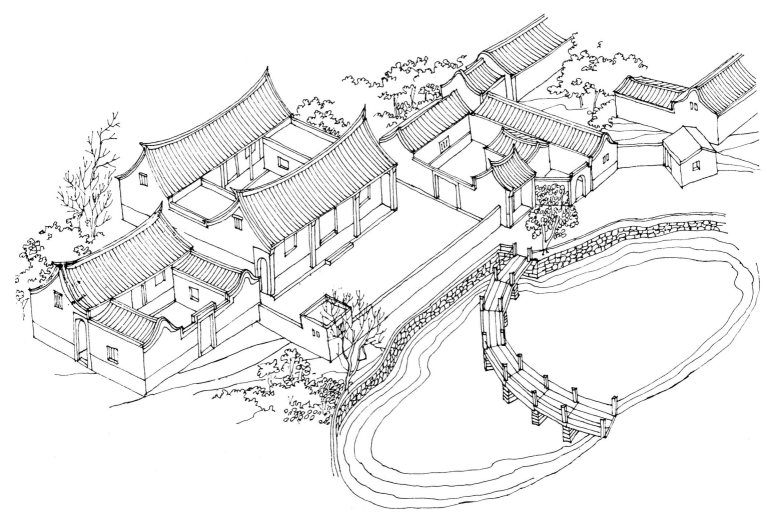

Traditionelle Architektur von Kinmen
(Quemoy).

Traditional architecture of Kinmen
(Quemoy).

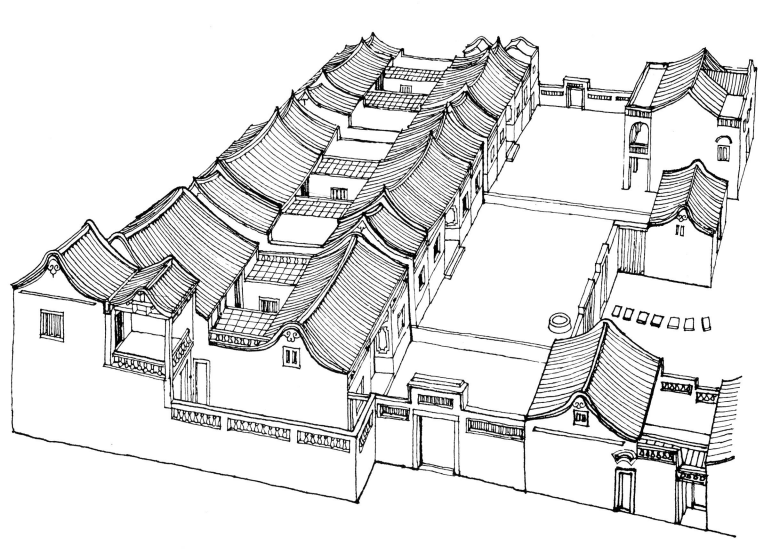

Der leere Raum in der klassischen
Architektur Japans

Die Teehaus-Tempel sind von der zen-
tralen Tempelanlage meist durch
mannshohe Mauern abgegrenzt, die
ein Ziegeldach schützt. An Stelle der
Mauern finden sich auch schöne Bam-
buszäune und dichte Hecken. Auf kleinen Pfaden, mit Steinplatten belegt, die
einem ganz bestimmten Schrittrhyth-
mus zugemessen sind, gelangt man in
die Nebenanlage. Es entspricht ganz
und gar jener feinen japanischen
Zurückhaltung, dass sich der einstök-
kige Holzbau so dem Naturbild einord-
net, dass lediglich der Eingang als ein
Teil der Gartenanlage ins Auge fällt,
während der Bau als solcher gar nicht
beachtet zu werden braucht. Deutlich
kommt diese Zurückhaltung auch in der
leichten Krümmung zum Ausdruck, die
jeder Pfad vor einem Eingang macht.
Hinter dieser Krümmung steht die
Absicht, all das, was hinter dem Eingang liegt, bescheiden zurückzuhalten.
Erst bei den letzten Schritten soll es
dem meditierend Daherschreitenden
sichtbar werden.
Die Gestaltung des japanischen Baus
geht von der Bodenmatte, der Tatami,
also vom Innenraum aus. Der Grundriss ergibt sich aus innenarchitektoni-
schen Gesichtspunkten. Doch der Raum
wird nicht durch vier starre Wände
gebildet, sondern durch die Leere, die
die stützenden und tragenden Holzbalken wie ein Rahmenwerk umgibt. Mit
Reispapier bespannte Schiebetüren
ermöglichen, die Räume voneinander
und nach aussen hin abzugrenzen. Sie
geben aber auch die Möglichkeit, diese
Begrenzungen aufzuheben, also den
Raum bis in den Garten zu erweitern
oder die einzelnen Räume ineinander
verschmelzen zu lassen.

The classical architecture of Japan and
empty space

The teahouse-temples are usually segre-
gated from the central temple complex
by man-high walls protected by a clay
tile coping. The walls are sometimes
replaced by fine bamboo fences or
dense hedges. Access to the teahouse
is by way of small paths paved with
stones which dictate a certain length of
step. It is consistent with Japanese deli-
cacy and restraint that the single-
storeyed wood building is so arranged
in the natural setting that only the
entrance strikes the eye as part of the
garden layout whereas the building as
such can be disregarded. The same
sense of restraint comes to the fore in
the slight curve each path describes in
front of an entrance. This curve is an
intimation of the intention of modestly
withholding from view everything
behind this entrance. It is only during the
last few steps that the visitor, approach-
ing in meditation, becomes aware of it.
The structure of the Japanese house is
determined by the floor mat, the tatami,
that is to say, from the inside outwards.
The plan is determined by factors of
interior architecture. However, the room
is not formed by the four rigid walls but
rather by the empty space which the
post-and-lintel timbers surround like a
cage. Sliding doors covered with rice
paper enable the rooms to be shut off
from each other and from outside. At
the same time they allow such partitions to be removed and the room to be
extended into the garden, or the individual rooms to be united in one.

88–103
Japanische Wohnpavillons mit symboli-
schen Gärten.

Japanese pavilions with symbolic
gardens.

89
Myôho-in Wohntempel mit kleinem
intimem Hof, Kyôto.

Myôho-in temple with small intimate
courtyard, Kyôto.

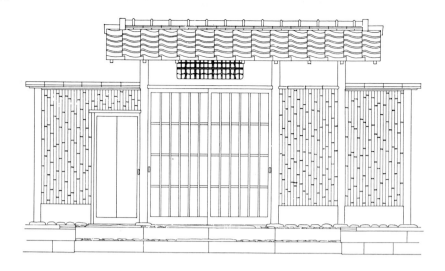

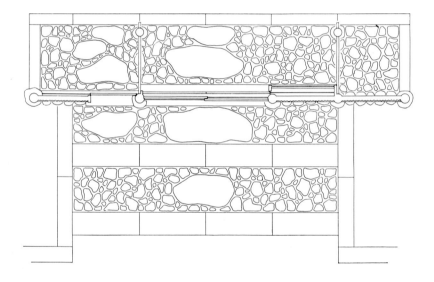

0   50   100 cm

90
Torhaus eines Landhauses, Massstab
1:50.

Gatehouse of a country house, scale
1:50.

91
Daisen-in, zen-buddhistisches Kloster
im Daitôku-ji-Tempelbezirk, Kyôto,
1509. Einswerden mit der Natur im
Steinhofgarten.

Daisen-in, Zen Buddhist monastery in
the Daitôku-ji temple complex, Kyôto,
1509. Unity with nature in the stone
garden.

92–93
Die Gartenhofwand wird in den Innenraum hinein projiziert.

The wall of the garden court is projected
into the interior.

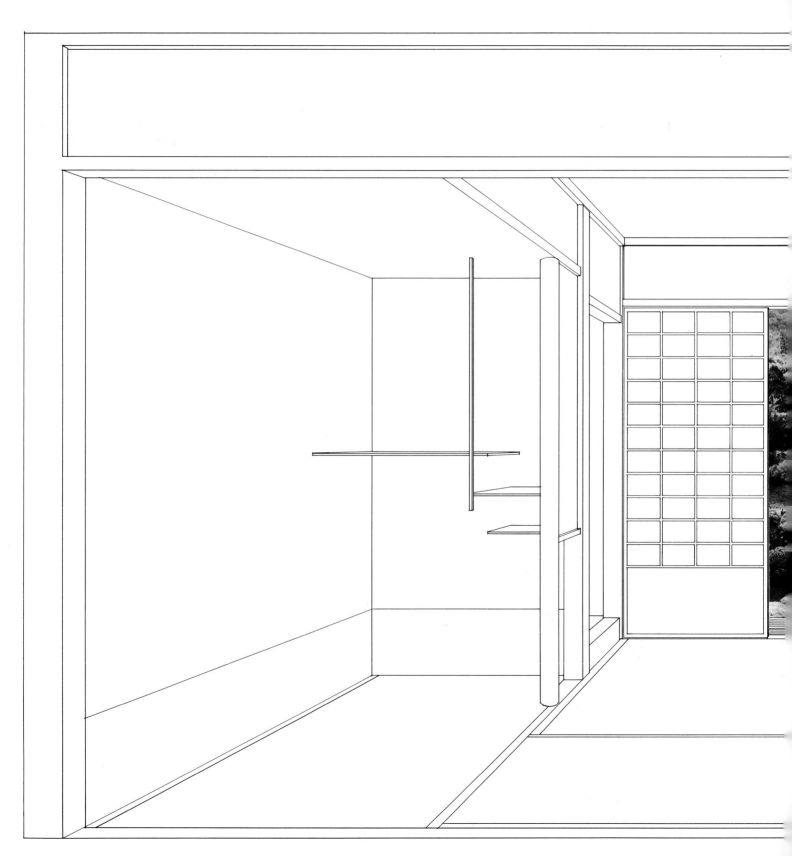

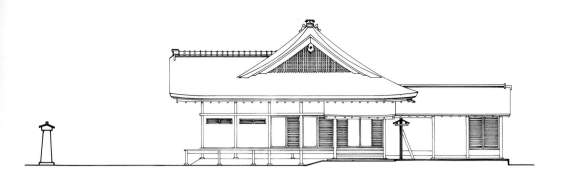

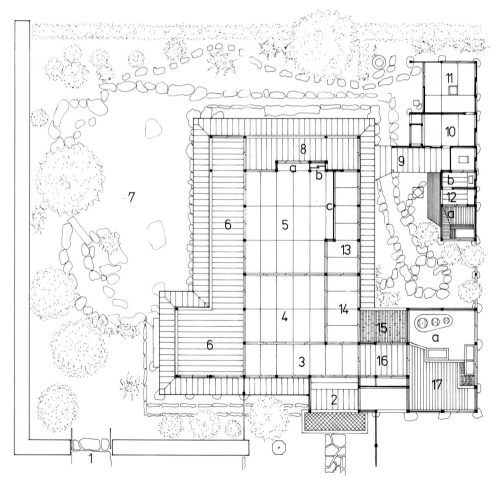

1 Garteneingang
  Garden entrance
2 Familieneingang
  Family entrance
3 Galerie
  Gallery
4 Zweiter Raum
  Second room
5 Erster Raum
  a – Tisch
  b – Regale
  c – Alkoven
  First room
  a – table
  b – shelves
  c – alcoves
6 Veranda
7 Garten
  Garden
8 Seitenveranda
  Side veranda
9 Brücke
  Bridge

10 Teehaus Waschraum
   Teahouse washroom
11 Teezeremonienraum
   Tea-ceremony room
12 Bad
   a – Hauptraum
   b – Toilette
   Bath
   a – main room
   b – toilet
13 Stauraum
   Storeroom
14 Galerie
   Gallery
15 Wirtschaftsveranda
   Working veranda
16 Waschküche
   Laundry
17 Küche (a = Herd)
   Kitchen

Typisches Beispiel für ein Gartenhofhaus, Massstab 1:200.

Typical example of a garden courtyard
house, scale 1:200.

95
Nijo-Schloss, Residenz der Tokugawa-
Shogune in Kyôto. Unterteilungswand
im Garten mit sichtbaren Holzbalken.

Nijo Castle, residence of the Tokugawa-
shoguns in Kyôto. Bayed partition wall
in the garden.

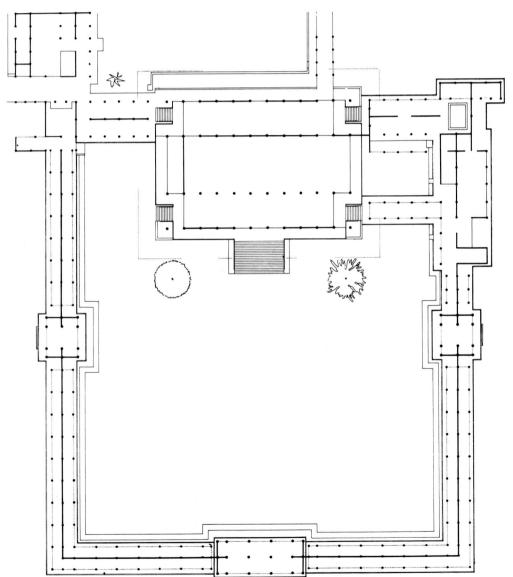

96–97
Kaiserlicher Kyôto-Palast Kogosho, Zer-
monienhalle des Kronprinzen. Bauten
aus der Mitte des 19. Jh. nach Plänen
aus dem 8. Jh.

Imperial Kyôto Palace, Kogosho, cere-
monial hall of the crown prince. Structures built in the mid-19th cent. according to 8th cent. plans.

97
Gartenwand und Halle im Ständerbau.

Garden wall and post-and-beam hall.

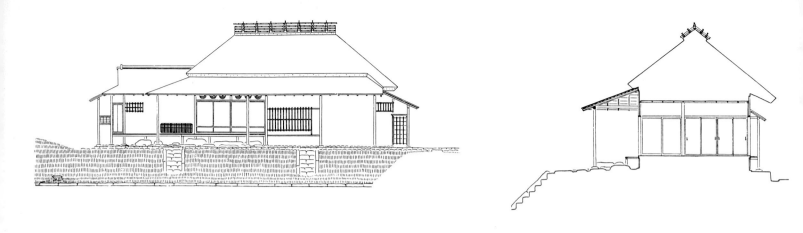

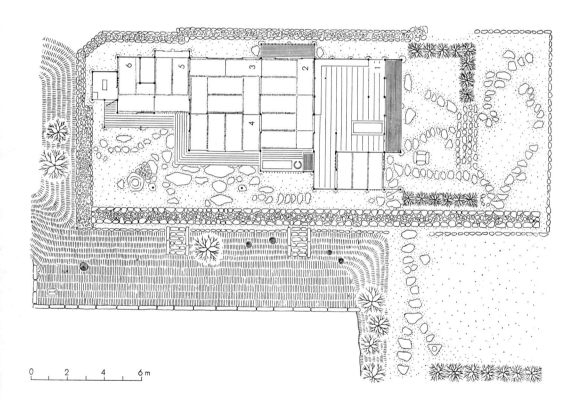

0   2   4   6 m

98
Teehaus Shôi-ken im Garten der kaiserlichen Katsura Villa, Kyôto, 1602.

Shôi-ken teahouse in the garden of the
imperial Katsura villa, Kyôto, 1602.

99
Ryôko-in, zen-buddhistisches Kloster im
Tempelbezirk des Daitôku-ji, Kyôto.
Wände innen und aussen; der Abt
Kobori Sohaku in seinem Kloster.

Ryôko-in, Zen Buddhist monastery in the
temple complex of Daitôku-ji, Kyôto.
Inside and outside walls: Abbot Kobori
Sohaku in his monastery.

Chugu-ji, buddhistisches Nonnenkloster bei Nara. Gehen im bewussten Rhythmus mit der Wandgliederung.

Chugu-ji, Buddhist nunnery near Nara. The pace is determined by the pattern of the wall.

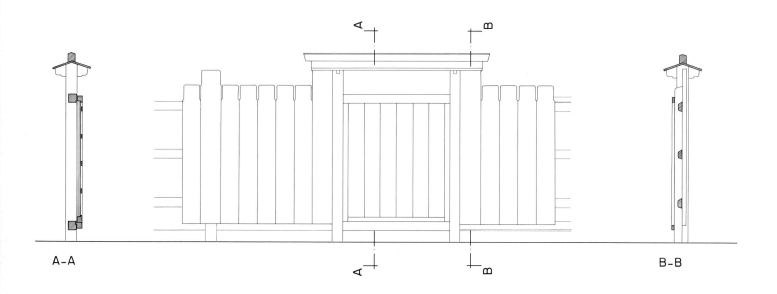

A–A   A   B   B–B

Ise-Schrein in Iseshi, Bautyp etwa aus dem 5. Jh. Der Hof im Shinto-Heiligtum darf nicht betreten werden. Ein mit einer Umzäunung geschlossener Hof – ohne Funktion, nur mit Symbol-Charakter. Massstab 1:50.

Ise shrine in Iseshi, archetypal structure dating from c. 5th cent. No one may enter the courtyard in the Shinto sanctuary. A courtyard enclosed by a fence and of only symbolic character. Drawing on scale 1:50.

Rurale Hofhaustypen

Bei der ruralen Architektur sind in der Regel Gebautes und Gewachsenes sowie Konstruktion und Material als Einheit erlebbar. Auf die jeweiligen Typen der bäuerlichen Haus- und Hofformen zurückzugreifen und daraus Bezüge zur heutigen Architektur abzuleiten, kann angesichts ihrer regionalen Vielfalt beispielhaft sein. Im Wort Bauernhof, in dem Wohn- und Wirtschaftsgebäude um einen Hof gruppiert sind, ist das Hofhaus schon miteinbezogen. Auf knappem Raum bilden die einzelnen Gebäude ein zusammenhängendes Ganzes, in dem jedes Glied, dank dem Innenhof, ein Höchstmass an Eigenständigkeit erhält.

Rural types of courtyard house

In rural architecture, as a rule, what is built and what grows seem to be one, and construction and material merge one into the other. In our quest for models, we might do well to look back at the various types of house and courtyard found in the country, particularly in view of their regional diversity, and see what lessons they have to teach for modern architecture. In the farmhouse where living quarters and service-related facilities are grouped round a yard we find another prototype of the courtyard house. United in a narrow space the individual buildings form an interrelated whole in which each element, because of the inner courtyard, acquires the maximum independence.

Mauerumschlossene Gehege auf der Aran-Insel Inisheer (Irland)

Ein Rasternetz von Steinwällen auf Inisheer dient den Haustieren als Unterkunft. Mit der Anpassung des Massstabs und der Materie an die Umgebung wird die Qualität des Bauwerkes sichtbar. Stein auf Stein bilden Hofgruppen über die weite Inselebene.

Walled enclosures on the Aran island of Inisheer (Ireland)

A network of drystone walls on Inisheer provides shelter for domestic animals. The quality of the structural work is evident in the adaptation of scale and material to the environment. All over the island stone has been placed on stone to form enclosures and the farm buildings are united with them to form a single structure.

Aran-Insel Inisheer (Irland). Mannshohe
Steingehege für die Behausung der
Tiere.

Aran island of Inisheer (Ireland).
Drystone walling as high as a man for
housing animals.

Dreiseithof in Altmünster bei Gmunden am Traunsee, etwa um 1780 (heute umfunktioniert zum Wohnhaus Raftl durch Architekt Johannes Spalt, Wien).

Haus Raftl ist ein typischer oberösterreichischer Dreiseithof mit Toreinfahrt an der Seeseite, wobei innerhalb dieses Dreiseithofes auf der einen Seite das Wohnhaus (zweigeschossig bewohnt), und anschliessend die Ställe, wie Kuhstall, Schweinestall und Pferdestall sich befinden. Weiter gehören zum Ensemble eine grosse Tenne mit Heuböden links und rechts, 2 Tore auf der Aussenseite und 2 Tore auf der Hofseite, sowie ein Werkstätten- und Holzraum, anschliessend an die dritte Seite und vom Hof aus zugänglich ist das Auszugshaus (Altenteilhaus), mit Zimmer und Küche ebenerdig. Im Hof befindet sich der Brunnen; das Dach ist mit selbstgefertigten Zementplatten abgedeckt und war früher mit Holzschindeln versehen.

A farmhouse of the 'three-sided' kind, built c. 1780, at Altmünster near Gmunden on the Traunsee, converted into a residence for the Raftl family by Johannes Spalt, architect, Vienna.

The Raftl House is a typical Upper Austrian 'Dreiseithof' with a carriage gateway on the side facing the lake. Within the three-sided courtyard there is on one side the two-storey house, which is the residential part, and next to it the cowshed, pigsty and stables. The complex also includes a large threshing-floor with haylofts to left and right, with two gateways on the outside and two gateways on the courtyard side, along with a workshop and wood store, and then, with access from the courtyard, there are the quarters comprising a room and kitchen for the retired farmer. The well is in the courtyard. The roof is covered with custom-made cement tiles instead of the original wood shingles.

106–109
Dreiseithof in Altmünster bei Gmunden am Traunsee, Oberösterreich um 1780.

'Dreiseithof' at Altmünster near Gmunden on Traunsee, Upper Austria, c. 1780.

Typischer Dreiseithof, Grundriss Erdgeschoss, Massstab 1:125.

Typical 'Dreiseithof', plan of ground floor, scale 1:125.

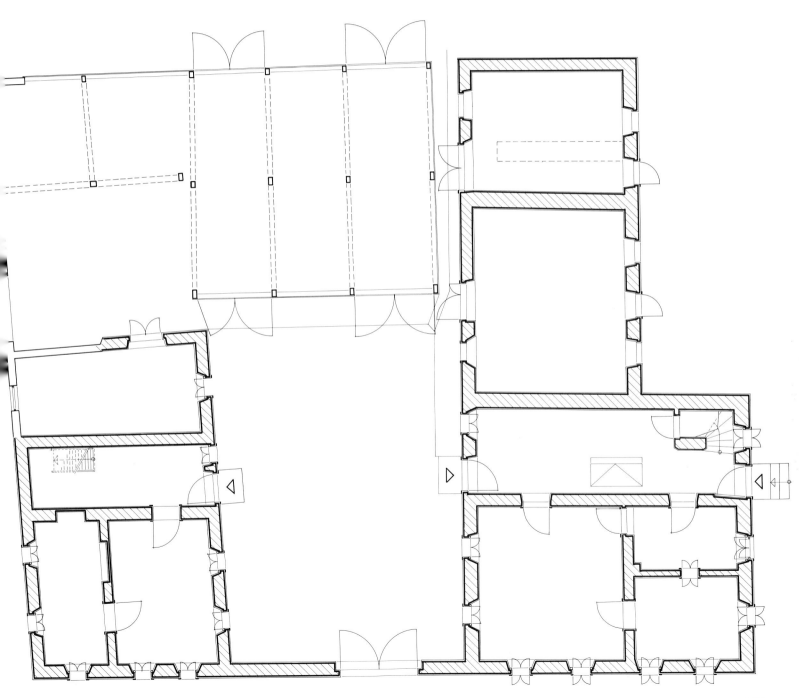

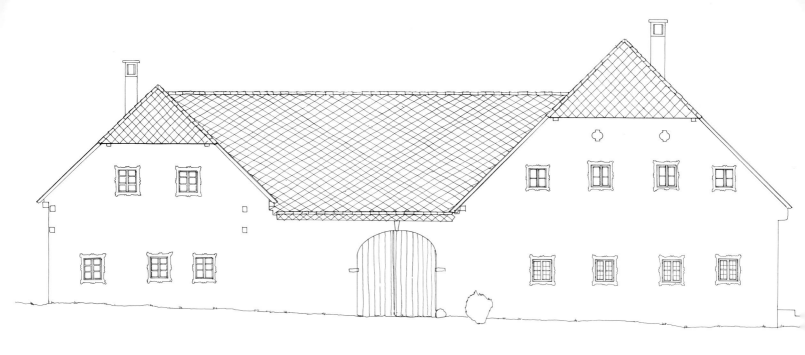

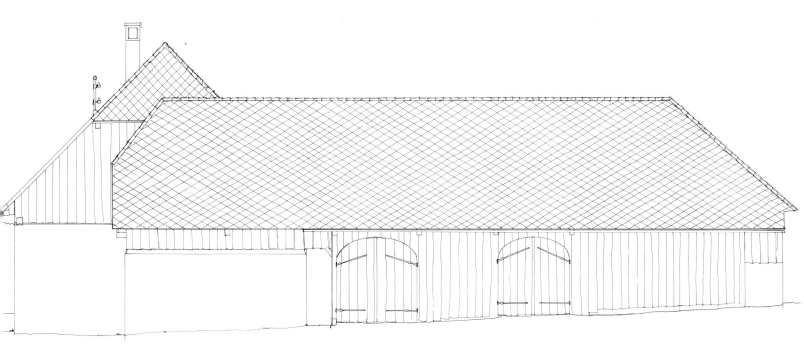

Ansichten und Schnitte, Massstab
1:125. Heutige Nutzung: Wohnhaus
Raftl.

Elevations and sections, scale 1:125.
Present use: Raftl House.

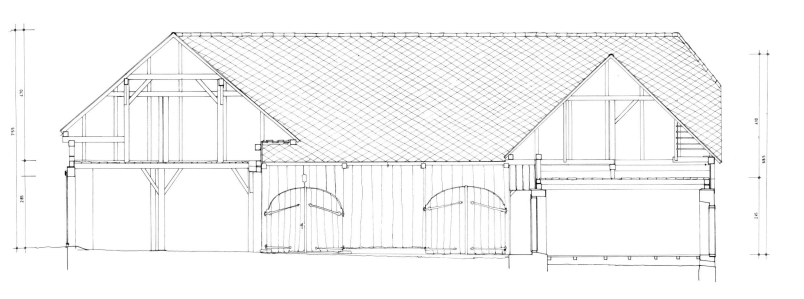

Dreiseit- und Vierkant-Hof in Österreich

Die bedeutendste Gehöftbildung in Österreich ist der Vierkanthof. Vier weitgehend gleichförmige Gebäudetrakte (bezüglich Länge, Höhe, Tiefe) gruppieren sich um einen nahezu quadratischen Innenhof. Diese vollkommene Gehöftform geht auf eine Entwicklung von über 600 Jahren zurück: ein Einhaus mit zentralem Hof, wobei alle Wege möglichst kurz und rationell sind. Das äussere Merkmal des Vierkanters liegt in der viertaktigen Anlage, bei dem Wohnhaus und Wirtschaftsgebäude in einem Baukörper vereinigt sind. Die geschlossene Firstlinie verbindet alle vier Trakte, also Wohnhaus, Stallgebäude, Tenne und Eingangspartie mit dem Tor zu einem gemeinsamen Dach.

Farmhouses in Austria

The most important forms of farmstead layout in Austria are the so-called three-sided and square farms (Dreiseithof and Vierkanthof). Four more or less uniform buildings (in respect of length, height and depth) are grouped round an almost square inner yard. This layout goes back 600 years: essentially it is a farmhouse with stables all under one roof round a central yard affording the shortest and most efficient routes between the buildings. Externally this layout is notable for the four-block arrangement in which the dwelling house and utility buildings form a unit. The house, stables, stalls and haylofts and the entrance section with its gateway form a common roof surface.

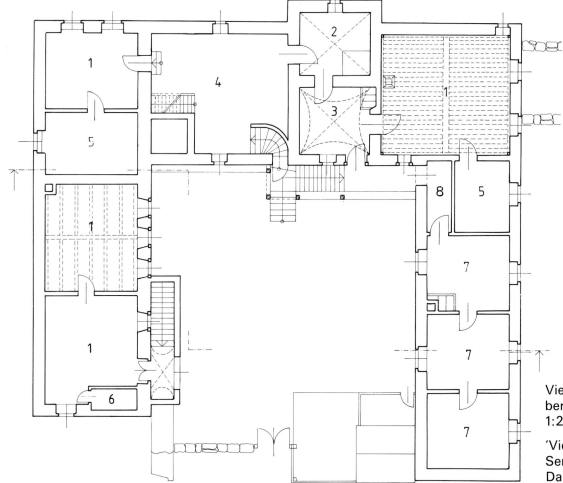

Vierkanthof, Haus Fischer, in Senftenberg bei Krems an der Donau, Massstab 1:200.

'Vierkanthof' now Fischer House, at Senftenberg near Krems on the Danube, scale 1:200.

1 Einfahrt
  Entrance
2 Obstkammer
  Fruit store
3 Vorkeller
  Front cellar
4 Zimmer
  Room
5 Kammer
  Box room
6 Kuhstall
  Cowshed
7 Düngerhaufen
  Dung heap
8 Schweinekoben
  Pigsty
9 Kuhstall
  Cowshed
10 Stall
   Stable

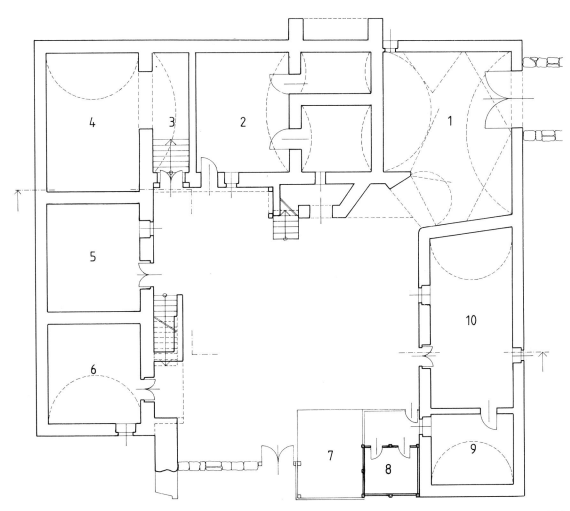

Hof-Häuser im Burgenland (Österreich)

Courtyard houses in Burgenland (Austria)

Die ruralen Bauten im Nordburgenland, einer Landschaft mit weiten Ebenen und karger Vegetation am Neusiedler See, sind dreiseitig von Gebäuden und der Eingangsfront, dem Tor umschlossen. Gegenüber dem Eingangstor ist das Wirtschaftstor in direkter Beziehung zur Landwirtschaft.

The rural buildings in north Burgenland, an area of broad plains and sparse vegetation on the Neusiedler See, consist of courtyards enclosed on three sides by buildings and the entrance including the gateway. Opposite the entrance is the farm gate leading directly to the fields.

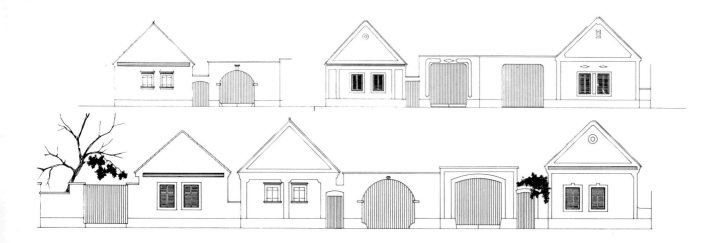

Ökonomie- und Wohnhof in Mörbisch, Burgenland (Österreich) Massstab 1:250.

Farmhouse and yard at Mörbisch, Burgenland (Austria), scale 1:250.

Fränkisches Gehöft mit Toranlage

Das fränkische Gehöft kommt meist im Dorfverband vor, in dem das Wohnhaus fast immer an der Dorfstrasse liegt. Den strassenseitigen Abschluss des Hofes bildet die Toranlage oder ein Torhaus. Der hintere Hofabschluss ist die Scheune, die auch eine Durchfahrt zum Feld besitzt. Alle Gebäude sind nur vom Hof aus zugänglich und haben nach aussen hin nicht einmal Fenster, bis auf die Stube des Wohnhauses, die einen Ausblick auf Strasse und Hof ermöglicht. Auf der Seite wo keine Gebäude sind, schliessen Mauern oder Bäume den Hof ab.

Franconian farmstead with gateway

The Franconian farmstead is found most commonly in the nucleated settlements; the dwelling house almost invariably gives onto the street. The yard is closed off on the street side by a gateway or gatehouse. The rear of the yard is formed by a barn with a passage through to the fields. The buildings are accessible only from the yard and have no windows on the outside, apart from the living room of the house whose windows look onto the street and the yard. In the absence of buildings, walls or trees shut off the yard.

1 Wohnstube
Living room
2 Küche
Kitchen
3 Diele
Entrance hall
4 Gänsestall
Goose house
5 Schweinestall
Pigsty
6 Kuhstall
Cowshed
7 Tenne
Threshing-floor
8 Bansen
Bays
9 Futterraum
Fodder room
10 Schweinestall
Pigsty
11 Grünfutter
Green forage
12 Geräteraum
Tool room
13 Jungvieh, darüber Hühnerstall
Young stock, hennery above
14 Holzschuppen
Wooden shed
15 Brennerei
Distillery
16 Schlafstube
Bedroom
17 Kammer
Storeroom
18 Räucherkammer
Smoking chamber
19 Hof
Courtyard

Fränkisches Gehöft in Brandenoberndorf-Taunus, Massstab 1:200.

Franconian farmhouse at Brandenoberndorf-Taunus, scale 1:200.

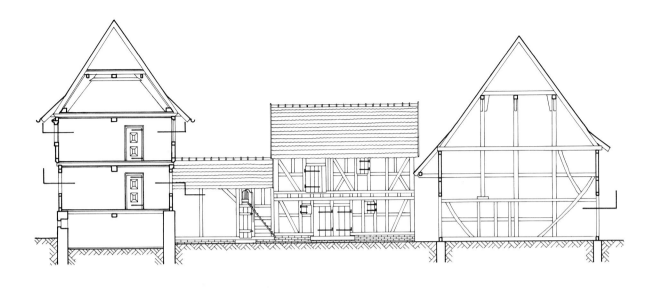

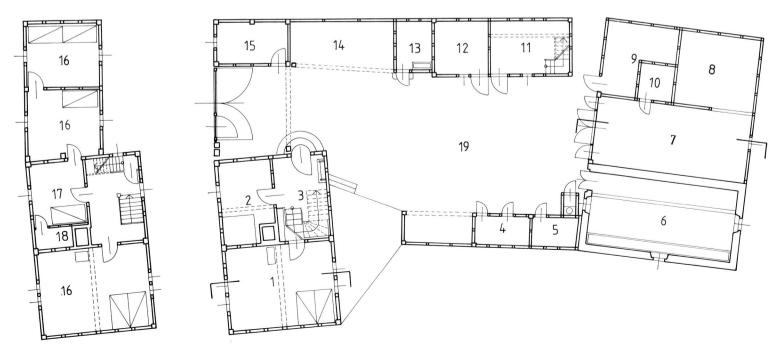

Delsbohof aus Hälsingland, anfangs 19. Jh. (heute in Skansen, Stockholm).

Delsbohof from Hälsingland, early 19th cent. (today at Skansen, Stockholm)

Der Delsbohof besteht aus sieben Gebäuden aus Hälsingland, alle aus – mit der Hand zugehauenen – Baumstämmen erbaut und mit einer fünffachen Lage Birkenrinde gedeckt, die von gespaltenen Stämmen festgehalten wird. Das Wohnhaus dagegen hat ein Ziegeldach. Nach alter nordischer Sitte sind fast alle Häuser dicht um einen viereckigen Hof gebaut. Im Gegensatz zu dem älteren Baustil sind alle anderthalb- oder zweistöckig. Das Gehöft hat zwei Wohnhäuser – eines für den Bauern und eines für seine alten Eltern. Beide sind gleich eingeteilt: in der Mitte der Hausflur, auf der einen Seite das Wohnzimmer und auf der anderen die gute Stube. Diese beiden Häuser wurden zu Anfang des 19. Jahrhunderts errichtet; die oberen Stockwerke wurden ungefähr im Jahr 1840, als die rote Farbe in Mode kam, gebaut. Auf der Westseite des Hofplatzes liegt ein zweistöckiges Gästehaus mit sechs Schlafräumen; daneben der Kuhstall mit hellen, getünchten Wänden und einem Lager für die Magd. Im grossen Haus mit der Einfahrt befinden sich der Pferdestall, die Scheune mit Tenne (Dreschboden) und ein geräumiger Heuboden. Ausserhalb der Hofanlage stehen zwei Vorratshäuser, die in Blockbautechnik auf vier Pfosten gebaut sind, damit Ratten und Mäuse nicht an die Vorräte herankönnen. (Aus Häuser und Höfe auf Skansen).

The Delsbohof is composed of seven buildings from Hälsingland, all of handhewn tree trunks and covered with a fivefold layer of birch bark held together by split sticks. The dwelling house, on the other hand, has a tiled roof. In accordance with an old Nordic custom, almost all the houses are built round a square courtyard. Unlike the older style of building, the houses all have one and a half or two storeys. The farmstead possesses two houses, one for the farmer and one for his old parents. Both are divided in the same way: in the middle the entrance hall, on one side the living room and on the other the parlour. Both these houses were built at the beginning of the 19th century; the upper storeys were added in 1840, when red became the fashionable colour. On the western side of the courtyard there is a two-storeyed guesthouse with six bedrooms; next to it the cowshed with light, whitewashed walls, and a room for the maid. In the large house containing the entrance are located the stables, the barn with the threshing floor, and a spacious hayloft. Outside the courtyard there are two log-built storehouses on four posts to keep out the rats and mice. (From 'Häuser und Höfe auf Skansen')

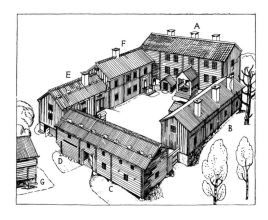

Der Delsbohof aus Hälsingland, heute im Freilichtmuseum, Skansen (Stockholm), Massstab 1:200.

The Delsbohof from Hälsingland, today in the Skansen open-air museum (Stockholm), scale 1:200.

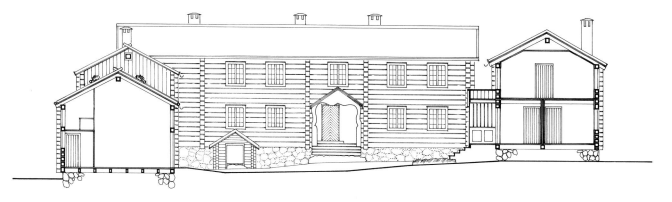

1 Diele
  Entrance hall
2 Wohnraum
  Living room
3 Stube
  Room
4 Stube
  Room
5 Gästezimmer
  Guest rooms
6 Kuhstall
  Cowshed
7 Scheune
  Barn
8 Pferdestall
  Stable
9 Durchfahrt
  Passage
10 Schuppen
  Shed
11 Brunnen
  Well
12 Hof
  Courtyard

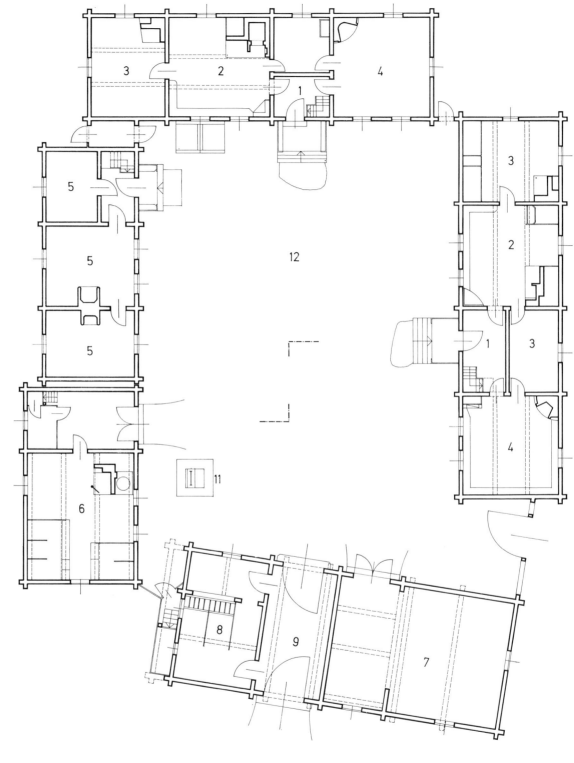

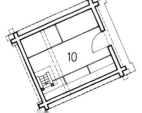

Einhegungen aus der Region Maramures (Rumänien)

Orthodoxe Holzkirchen des 17. und 18. Jahrhunderts und Bauernhäuser werden von geflochtenen Zäunen und prächtig geschmückten Toren umrahmt. Laubengänge unter dem Dachvorsprung der Gebäude stehen in Zusammenhang mit der Umhegung und bilden den privaten, intimen Hofbereich. Die Region Maramures im Norden des Landes ist heute noch ein Beispiel einer intakten Kultur seiner Bewohner mit ihrer hervorragenden Holzarchitektur.

Enclosures in the Maramures region (Rumania)

Orthodox timber churches of the 17th and 18th centuries and farmhouses are surrounded by wicker fences and splendidly decorated gates. Covered walks under the projecting eaves of the buildings are linked up with the enclosure and form the private courtyard area. The Maramures region in the north of the country still remains a model with the intact culture of its inhabitants and the magnificent timber architecture.

118–119
Holzbauten aus der Region Maramures (Rumänien). Geflochtener Zaun und Tor mit reichem Schnitzwerk aus dem Dorfe Satusgâtag (Maratal).

Timber buildings from the region of Maramures (Rumania). Wicker fence and gate with rich carvings from the village of Satusgâtag (Mara valley).

Bauernhof in Boxwiller (Elsass), 1780

Farmhouse at Bouxwiller (Alsace), 1780

Elsässische Häuser zeigen immer noch das altertümliche Bild einer reichen Kulisse von Fachwerkkonstruktionen mit originellen Riegelkombinationen. Das Dach schützt Giebel und Längsmauern und ist gegen die Hofseite weit ausladend. Einseitiges Vorherrschen des Weinbaus begünstigt die Erhaltung dieses Bautyps.

Alsatian houses still present the time-hallowed picture of wood framed constructions with ingenious patterns of half timbering. The roof protects the gable and the long walls and projects far over the courtyard. The predominance of vine cultivation has favoured the preservation of this type of building.

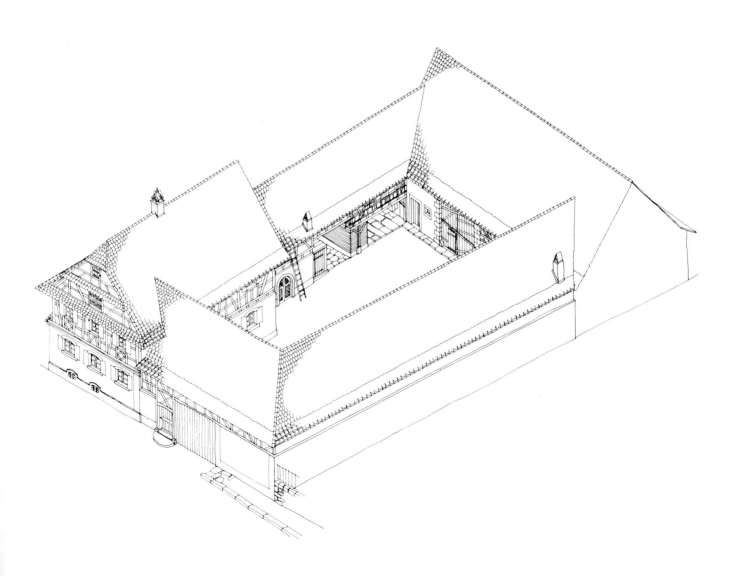

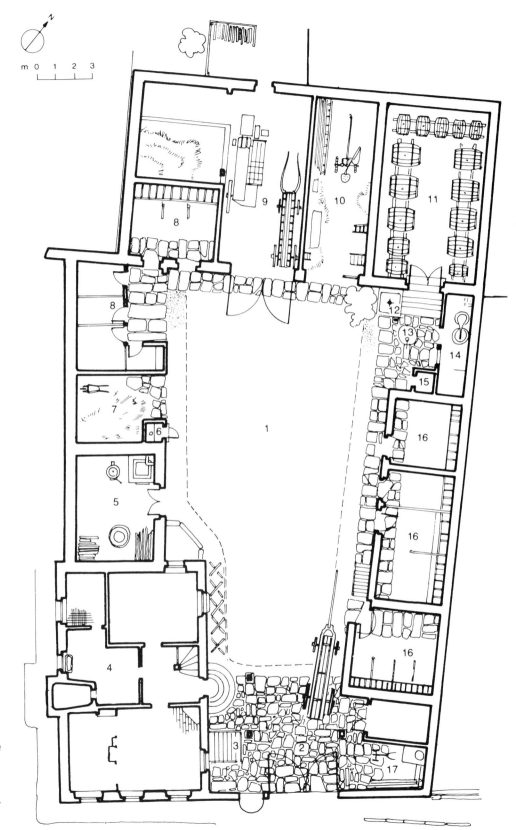

Bauernhof in Bouxwiller (Elsass) etwa
19. Jh. Allseitig umschliessen Gebäude
den Hofraum.

Farmhouse at Bouxwiller (Alsace)
c. 19th cent. The courtyard is surrounded on all sides by buildings.

Patios im Kolonialstil aus Salta,
Argentinien

Der Kolonialstil des spanischen Patio-
hauses, eine uralte lebensnotwendige
Einrichtung, entstand zwischen
1895–1930, als Einwanderergruppen
dazu neigten, ihre bauliche Tradition zu
erhalten. Im innerstädtischen Bereich
sind die Innenhöfe klein, von hohen
Mauern und breiten Dachüberständen
beschattet. Im allgemeinen dient der
Innenhof von Wohnhäusern in ländlicher Umgebung dazu, mehr Sonnen-
licht in das Haus eindringen zu lassen.
Das Verhältnis vom Innenhof zum Haus
richtet sich darum nach der umgebenden Behausung. Gartenhofhäuser von
heute basieren auf einer verdichteten
Wohnform. Die Abgeschlossenheit zum
Garten und die gute Orientierung zu den
Räumen waren die funktionalen Krite-
rien. Bepflanzte Patios mit Säulen sind
Elemente des offenen Binnenhofes der
spanischen und ibero-amerikanischen
Baukunst.

Patios in colonial style at Salta,
Argentina

The colonial style of the Spanish patio
house, an ancient layout designed to
meet living conditions, came into being
between 1895 and 1930, when groups
of immigrants were desirous of preserv-
ing their architectural tradition. Inside
the towns the inner courts are small,
shaded by high walls and deep eaves. In
general the inner courts of rural houses
serve to admit more sunshine into the
house. The relationship of the inner
court to the house is therefore governed
by the surrounding housing. Garden
courtyard houses of today are based on
high-density living. Enclosure on the
garden side and good orientation to the
rooms of the house are the functional
criteria. Planted patios with columns are
characteristic elements of the open
court in Spanish and Hispano-American
architecture.

122–131
Kolonialarchitektur aus Salta, Argentinien.

Colonial architecture at Salta, Argentina.

123
Eingang eines Architekturbüros im
innerstädtischen Bereich von Salta.

Entrance to an architect's office in the
centre of Salta.

Wohnhaus eines Zuckerrohrfarmers bei
Salta

Der Patio wird von allen Seiten durch
Rundsäulen auf quadratischen Sockeln
stehend gebildet. Die Vegetation erinnert an den mediterranen Hofraum.
Schlichte Architektur und additive Säu-
lenreihen geben dem Wohnpatio einen
starken Akzent.

House of a sugar-cane farmer
near Salta

The patio is formed on all sides by round
columns on square plinths. The planting
is reminiscent of the Mediterranean
courtyard. Simple architecture and additive rows of columns strongly accentu-
ate the living patio.

124–127
Wohnhaus eines Zuckerrohrfarmers bei
Salta.

House of a sugar-cane farmer near
Salta.

126–127
Typischer ländlicher Patio.

Typical country patio.

Finca Patrón Costa, Salta, 19. Jahrhundert (seit 1968 Mercado Artesanal)

Das früher feudale Wohnhaus besitzt einen pergolaähnlichen, mit umlaufenden, einfachen Holzsäulen geprägten, intimen Hofraum. Die Hauptfront wird von wuchtigen achteckigen Steinsäulen mit quadratischem Kapitell gebildet.

Finca Patrón Costa, Salta, 19th cent. (since 1968 Mercado Artesanal)

This former palatial residence has a pergola-like court surrounded by simple wooden pillars. The main front is formed of sturdy octagonal stone columns with square capitals.

128–129
Finca Patrón Costa, Salta 19. Jh., heute Mercado Artesanal.

Finca Patrón Costa, Salta, 19th cent., today Mercado Artesanal.

Haus an der Calle Caseros, Salta

Auf knappem Raum bietet der Patio im innerstädtischen Bereich ein Maximum an Wohnqualität. Der kleine Hof ist durch die farbige Scheibe mit pflanzlichen Jundstilmotiven von der Strasse her erkenntlich.

House in the Calle Caseros, Salta

Inside the town, where space is scarce, the patio affords the highest quality of living. The small court can be recognized from the street by the coloured panel with vegetal Art Nouveau motifs.

130–131
Haus an der Calle Caseros, Salta. Jugendstilhaustür von aussen und vom Patio.

House in the Calle Caseros, Salta. Art Nouveau door giving onto the street and patio.

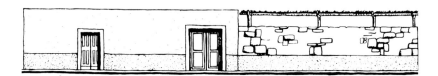

TECHOS DE LAMINA GALVANIZADA

SALA
ZAGUAN
PAJAR
BODEGA

MURO DE ADOBE

CIMIENTO DE ·PIEDRA
PISO DE CEMENTO
PISO DE TIERRA
PISO DE TIERRA

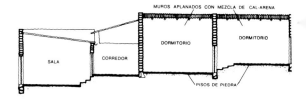

MUROS APLANADOS CON MEZCLA DE CAL-ARENA

DORMITORIO
DORMITORIO

SALA
CORREDOR

PISOS DE PIEDRA

Ländliche Architektur aus México.
Wohnräume um einen Patio, Dächer
mit Ziegeln belegt.

Rural architecture in Mexico. Living
rooms round a patio, tiled roofs.

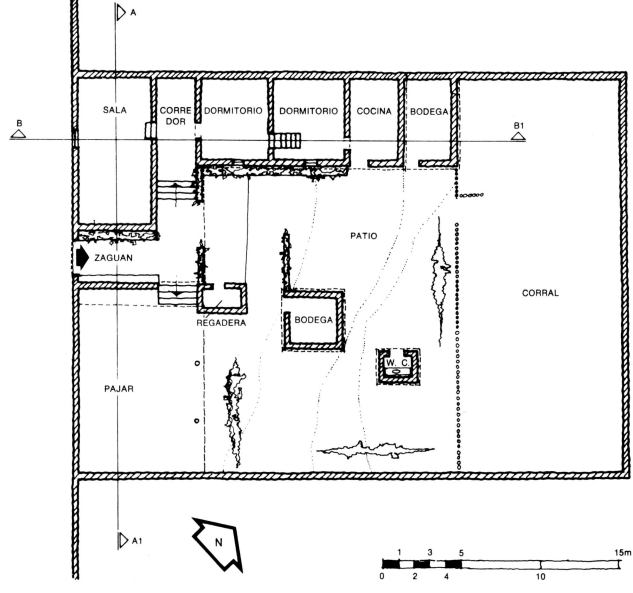

SALA

CORRE
DOR

DORMITORIO

DORMITORIO

COCINA

BODEGA

A

B

B1

ZAGUAN

REGADERA

PATIO

BODEGA

W. C.

CORRAL

PAJAR

A1

N

| 1 | 3 | 5 | | 15m |

0   2   4   10

Kreuzgang, ein sakraler Hof

Im Zentrum der Klosteranlage liegt der Kreuzgang: Ein gewölbter Gang, der um einen viereckigen, mit Grün bepflanzten Innenhof gelegt ist. Im Kreuzgang sind wir vor der Hektik und dem Lärm der Aussenwelt geschützt. Helligkeit und Dunkelheit im gedeckten und offenen Bereich laden zur Meditation und Stille ein. Jeder Hof hat auch einen formalen d.h. einen ästhetischen Aspekt. Nach Vitruvius ist die Proportion ‹die Harmonie der verschiedenen Bestandteile mit dem Ganzen›.

Cloisters – ecclesiastical courtyards

In the centre of the monastery layout is the cloister, a vaulted walk round a square court planted with greenery. In the cloister we feel remote from the noise and bustle of the world, and the alternating light and shade of the open and covered areas is conducive to meditation and tranquillity. Each courtyard also has its formal or aesthetic aspect. According to Vitruvius, proportion is the harmonization of the various components with the whole.

Zisterzienser-Abtei Fontenay, Burgund, 1129–1147

Die Baukunst der Zisterzienser war demonstrativ einfach gehalten. Diese Einfachheit ist im Grundriss und Aufriss erkennbar. Die früheste völlig erhaltene Kirche ist die von Fontenay, die grösste ist Pontigny (etwa 1140–1200), ebenfalls im Burgund.

Cistercian abbey at Fontenay, Burgundy, 1129–47

Cistercian architecture was kept deliberately simple. This simplicity can be recognized in the plan and elevation. The earliest still fully preserved church in Burgundy is that of Fontenay, the largest is Pontigny (c. 1140–1200).

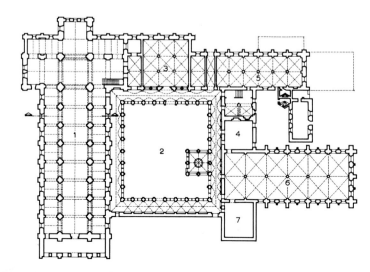

Zisterzienser-Abtei Fontenay, im Burgund, Abtei und Kreuzhof sind in gutem Zustand.

Cistercian abbey at Fontenay, in Burgundy. The abbey and the cloister are in a good state of preservation.

Kreuzgang des Klosters von Saint-Trophime, Arles, 10. Jahrhundert

Der graziöse Kreuzhof, um 1190 erbaut, ist mit seinem überwölbten Gang einer der schönsten dieser Art.

Cloister in the monastery of Saint Trophime, Arles, 10th cent.

The gracious cloister c. 1190 with its vaulted walk is one of the most beautiful of its kind.

136–139
Kloster Saint-Trophime in Arles.

Saint Trophime monastery at Arles.

138–139
Formaler und ästhetischer Aspekt von Innenhof und Kreuzgang.

Formal and aesthetic aspect of the inner court and cloister.

San Lorenzo fuori le Mura, Rom,
12. Jahrhundert

In den romanischen Bauten ist die
Wand zugleich der Träger, doch kommt
die Zerlegung in durchgehende Stützen
und nur füllende Wandteile vielfach vor;
deutlich wird dies bei den Pfeilern der
Arkaden in Kreuzgängen sichtbar.

San Lorenzo fuori le Mura, Rome,
12th cent.

In Romanesque buildings the wall is
also the load-bearing element but there
are frequent examples in which the
load is distributed over continuous
columns and the wall is simply infilling:
this is clearly the function of the
columns in the arcades of these clois-
ters.

140–141
San Lorenzo fuori le Mura, in Rom.
Innenhof mit pflanzlichem Charakter.

San Lorenzo fuori le Mura, Rome. Inner
court with planting.

Cortile von San Carlo alle quattro
Fontane, Francesco Borromini, Rom,
1634–1641

Die Kirche ist ein Frühwerk Borrominis
in barocker Linienführung. Die Eleganz
des italienischen Barocks beruht auf
der Beziehung von Säule, Bogen, Pilaster und Giebel, auch wo diese Struktur
durch reiche Ornamentierung verschlei-
ert wird. Der kleine mehrstöckige
Innenhof besteht aus symmetrischen
Rundbogenöffnungen.

Cortile of San Carlo alle quattro Fontane,
Francesco Borromini, Rome, 1634–41

This church is one of Borromini's early
works in which an organic line is apparent in the design. The elegance of Italian Baroque depends on the relationship of pillar, arch, pilaster and gable,
even where these structures are
obscured by rich ornamentation. The
small multistorey inner court has walls
in which symmetrical round-arched
openings are repeated.

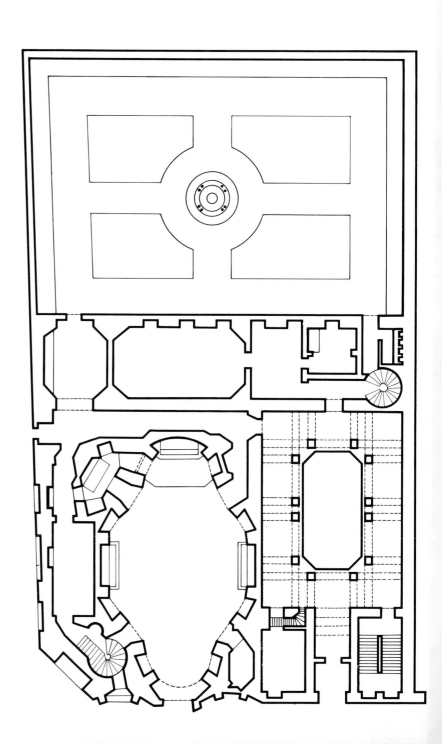

San Carlo alle quattro Fontane in Rom,
Kleiner intimer Innenhof.

San Carlo alle quattro Fontane, Rome.
Small intimate inner court.

Palazzo della Cancelleria, ein Meisterwerk der Frührenaissance, Rom,
1483–1511

Sehenswert ist der Hof, in den Bramante
wahrscheinlich die 44 antiken Säulen
aus der alten Basilika des heiligen Lau-
rentius in Damaso einbaute. Der drei-
geschossige Hof hat Säulenhallen von
unübertrefflicher Formenklarheit mit
einer höchst knapp profilierten Traver-
tinfassade. Dieses Bauwerk der Frührenaissance zeigt mit den schlanken
Rundbögen ein Gleichmass von Gliederung und Proportion.

Palazzo della Cancelleria, a masterpiece
of the Early Renaissance, Rome,
1483–1511

The courtyard is particularly worth see-
ing with its 44 antique columns. Bramante probably used the columns from
the old basilica of S. Lorenzo in Damaso. The three-storeyed court has colonnades of unparalleled formal clarity
with a barely modelled facade of trav-
ertine. With its slender rounded arches,
this Early Renaissance building brings
articulation and proportion into a just
balance.

144–145
Palazzo della Cancelleria in Rom. Arkaden und Fassade mit rhythmischer Säu-
lenführung.

Palazzo della Cancelleria, Rome.
Arcades and facade with rhythmic
spacing of columns.

Hofhäuser des 20. Jahrhunderts

Hofhaus als Ensemble: Das Hofhaus ist durch seinen unverwechselbaren Stil der horizontalen Architektur und durch die einmalige Geschlossenheit der Konzeption geprägt. Nicht das Einzelgebäude sondern die Baugruppe bildet die grundlegende architektonische Einheit. Das Einzelgebäude mit seinem gegliederten Hof ist eingebunden in den grösseren Zusammenhang eines Hofensembles.

Bewohntes Zimmer: Im urbanen Siedlungsverband erhöht ein Hof die Wohnqualität. Er bildet einen Freiraum mit intimem Charakter und dient als Zentrum des Hauses; im Sommer als bewohntes Zimmer, im Winter als Verbindung zwischen Mensch und Natur, weil er die wechselnden Jahreszeiten in das Haus einlässt. Die Benützer sind gegen Einblicke, Wind und Lärm geschützt.

Besiedlungsdichte: Das Hofhaus nimmt Rücksicht auf die Anforderung der Besiedlungsdichte. Sein Verdienst ist es, die Beziehung zwischen Haus und Hof in gesunder, preisgünstiger und dichter Bauweise zu integrieren. Die Verflechtung dieses Baukonzeptes mit mehrgeschossigen Mietwohnhäusern mit ihrem oft uniformen, dem Individuum nicht gerecht werdenden Charakter, könnte eine natürlichere Wohnform ergeben.

Lichtspender: Gerade in unserer Zeit wird der Wunsch nach dem Lichtspender eines Atriums als individuelle Freiheit angesehen. Zum Beispiel bedeutet heute noch in Griechenland das Wort Atrium (Aithrius Ouvranòs) ‹klarer Himmel›. In der Kleinstadt und auf kleinen Grundstücken könnte durch den Aspekt der Rationalisierung und die Idee der Ausnützung von Fläche und Raum dieses Bausystem wieder auf wachsendes Interesse stossen. Das frühere repräsentative Wohnen wird nicht mehr akzeptiert. Hingegen bleibt aber der Einfallsreichtum in der Gliederung des Grundrisses für unser Bauen erhalten.

Courtyard houses of the 20th century

The courtyard house as a complex: The courtyard house is characterized by the obligate style of horizontal architecture and the unprecedented unity of the design. The basic architectural unit is not the individual building but the group. The single building with its structured court is integrated into the larger context of the courtyard complex. This is an eminently sensible arrangement.

An extra room to live in: In the dense pattern of urban settlement a courtyard enhances the quality of life. It provides an open-air room of an intimate character and serves as the nucleus of the house; in summer it is an extra room to live in, in winter it is a link between man and nature, bringing the changing seasons into the heart of the house. Those living there are protected from noise, overlooking and wind.

Density of settlement: The courtyard house takes cognizance of density needs. Its great merit is that it integrates house and court in a health-giving, compact design at low cost. In contrast to multistorey blocks of flats with their often uniform character, which is little adapted to individual needs, the interlinking of houses designed on these lines produces a natural form of living.

Source of light: Especially in these days the desire for the atrium as a source of light is interpreted in terms of personal freedom. For example, the word for atrium in Greece (aithrius ouvranòs) means 'clear sky'. In small towns and on restricted lots the rational nature of this system, and the maximum use it makes of the available space, is calculated to elicit growing interest. At the same time the arrangement of the plan affords ample scope for ingenuity of design.

Heinrich Tessenow, Berlin, 1876–1950

Tessenows geistige Herkunft aus den Arts and Crafts ist in der Landhauskolonie Neu-Dölau bei Halle an der Saale deutlich zu sehen: Typische Formelemente mit glatten Flächen und berankte Laubengänge als halböffentliche Bereiche vor den Eingängen. Der Verzicht auf jeglichen Pathos charakterisiert seine sensiblen, inspirierten ‹Hof›-Zeichnungen.

Heinrich Tessenow, Berlin, 1876–1950

Tessenow's intellectual origins in arts and crafts are apparent in the rural house development at Neu-Dölau near Halle on the Saale. Typical formal elements are the flat spaces and creeper-covered walks as semi-public areas in front of the entrances. His sensitive 'courtyard' drawings show characteristically how he has avoided any emotionalism.

147–149
Heinrich Tessenow, Ideenskizzen, Wien um 1916.

Heinrich Tessenow, sketches, Vienna, c. 1916.

147
Traditionelle deutsche Kleinhaussiedlung.

Traditional German estate of small houses.

148
Blumenlattenwände von 3,50 m Höhe umschliessen die Eingangsfront.

Lattice walls 3.50 m high surround the entrance.

149
Brunnenhof eines Gutsherrenhauses in Norddeutschland.

Fountain court of a landowner's house in north Germany.

Hofhausprojekte, Mies van der Rohe, Berlin 1931–1938

Ludwig Mies van der Rohe durchbrach das Konzept einer Villa, indem er auf einen Teil der geschosshohen umlaufenden Backsteinwand eine Dachplatte legte und somit die Beziehung zwischen Haus und Hof verfeinerte. Unter dem Dach im Innern befinden sich vielfach keine abgeschlossenen Räume, sondern Bereiche. Der innere Hof schützt vor Wind und verbindet Innen mit Aussen.

Courtyard house projects, Mies van der Rohe, Berlin 1931–38

Ludwig Mies van der Rohe got away from the concept of the villa by placing a roof slab on part of the storey-high enclosing brick wall, thus refining the relationship between house and courtyard. Under the roof in the interior there are often areas rather than enclosed rooms. The inner court keeps out the wind and makes for a close indoor-outdoor link.

Der Deutsche Pavillon auf der Weltausstellung in Barcelona, von Mies van der Rohe, Berlin, 1929

Der Pavillon schliesst nichts als Raum ein und dies erst noch in einer geometrischen und keineswegs wirklichen oder physischen Weise. Er besitzt keine Türen und, noch mehr, jeder Saal ist nur unvollkommen abgeschlossen, z.B. auf drei Seiten durch drei Scheidewände. Diese sind meist fortlaufende, grosse Glasscheiben, die den Raum nur teilweise begrenzen. Manche dieser Scheiben sind von dunkler und neutraler Färbung und spiegeln die Dinge und die Leute, sodass das, was Sie durch die Scheiben sehen, sich mit den Spiegelbildern verwirrt. In einigen Sälen fehlt die Decke: das sind richtige demi-Patios, in denen der Raum nur durch drei Mauern und die horizontale Oberfläche des Wassers im Bassin beschränkt, aber durch die Geometrie festgehalten wird.
Wenn Sie sich dem Pavillon nähern und dann, wenn Sie in ihn eintreten, sind Sie erstaunt durch diesen Eindruck des Unzweckmässigen, der durch diese offenen und leeren Säle, diese schönen, nackten und öden Marmorwände und durch diese unbewohnbaren Patios hervorgerufen wird; und Sie verspüren dabei den Angriff der, wenn ich sagen darf, übersinnlichen Architektur.

The German Pavilion at the Barcelona world exhibition by Mies van der Rohe, Berlin, 1929

The pavilion encloses nothing but space, not in a real or physical sense but as an exercise in geometrical composition. It has no doors, and what is more, each room is only incompletely enclosed, say, on three sides by three partitions. The walls are mainly large continuous sheets of glass which define the space only in part. Some of these sheets are dark or neutral in colour and reflect objects and people, so that what you see through the glass is obscured by reflections. In some rooms there is no ceiling: these are real demi-patios in which space is bounded only by three walls and the horizontal surface of the water; they are spaces held in a cage of geometry.
When you approach and then when you enter the pavilion, you are struck by the impression of impracticality created by the open and empty rooms, the beautiful marble walls, bare and unadorned, and by these uninhabitable patios; and you feel the impact of what I may call suprasensuous architecture. (From Cahiers d'Art, 1929)

150–167
Projekte für Hofhäuser von Mies van der Rohe, Berlin und Chicago.

Projects for courtyard houses by Mies van der Rohe, Berlin and Chicago.

151–153
Deutscher Repräsentationsbau auf der Weltausstellung in Barcelona, 1929.

German prestige building at the world exhibition in Barcelona, 1929.

151
Im Wasserhof, einem Demi-Patio, steht die Plastik von Georg Kolbe.

Demi-patio with a sculpture by Georg Kolbe.

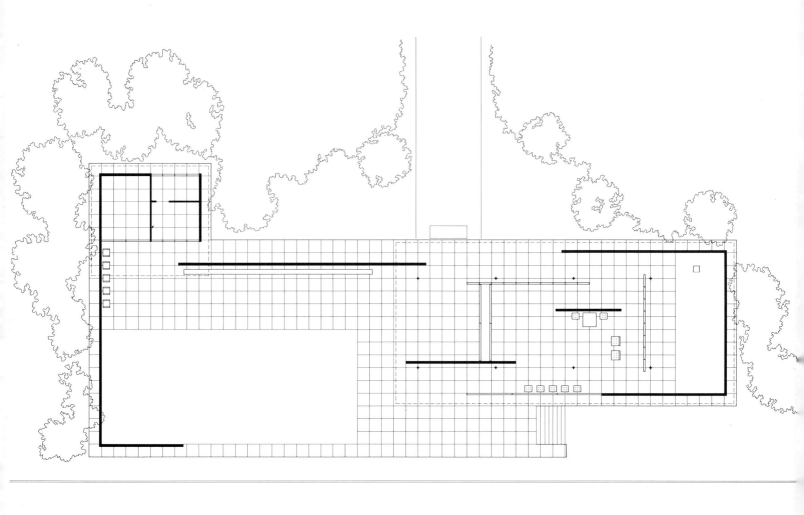

152
Grundriss des Pavillons, Massstab
1:300.

Plan of the pavilion, scale 1:300.

153
Die eingeschobenen Wände sind unab-
hängig von den tragenden Kreuzstüt-
zen.

The interior walls are independent of the
load-bearing cross-shaped steel pillars.

Ein-Bett-Atrium-Haus von Howard
Dearstyne, Bauhaus Dessau, 1931

Als Mies 1930 ans Bauhaus Dessau
kam, waren die Grundprinzipien seiner
Lehre durch sein Werk schon vorhanden, sodass seine Schüler damit experi-
mentieren konnten. Das Hofhaus als
Schulübung stand schon in den dreissiger Jahren im Mittelpunkt seiner Interessen. Ein Hofhaus-Projekt vom ameri-
kanischen Studenten Howard Dearstyne
(entwickelt während der Bauhauszeit in
Dessau 1931 unter Mies) zeigt eine
räumliche Lösung mit Backsteinwän-
den, die Haus und Hof umschliessen:
der Raum ist das Primäre, die Stellung
der Wände definiert ihn. Innen und
Aussen bilden ein Ganzes. Gerade das
Beispiel Hofhaus hat sich später in der
Arbeit seiner Schüler am IIT in Chicago
bis heute besonders intensiv durchge-
setzt. An diesem Problem kann die
systematische Architekturlehre ohne
allzu enge funktionelle Einengung klar
und anschaulich studiert werden: Das
Gesetz der Backsteinmauer, die nicht
tragende Innenwand, die Anordnung der
Möbel, die Auseinandersetzung mit
dem künstlerischen Bildschmuck und
die Festlegung von Konstruktion und
Raum.

One-bed atrium house by Howard
Dearstyne, Bauhaus Dessau, 1931

When Mies came to the Bauhaus in
Dessau in 1930, the basic principles of
his doctrine were already embodied in
his work and consequently his pupils
could use it for experiment. Even back in
the thirties, the courtyard house as an
academic exercise was already a central interest of his. A courtyard house
project produced by the American stu-
dent Howard Dearstyne during his time
at the Bauhaus with Mies provides for
brick walls enclosing the house and the
court: space is the primary element and
the position of the walls defines it.
Inside and outside form a whole. The
courtyard house has in fact continued
down to this day to figure prominently in
the work of his students at the IIT in
Chicago. It is a problem in which
systematic architectural doctrine can be
studied clearly and graphically without
any too narrow functional restriction:
the law of the brick wall, the non-bear-
ing internal wall, the arrangement of
furniture, the question of artistic pictorial
decoration, and the determination of
construction and space.

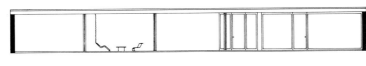
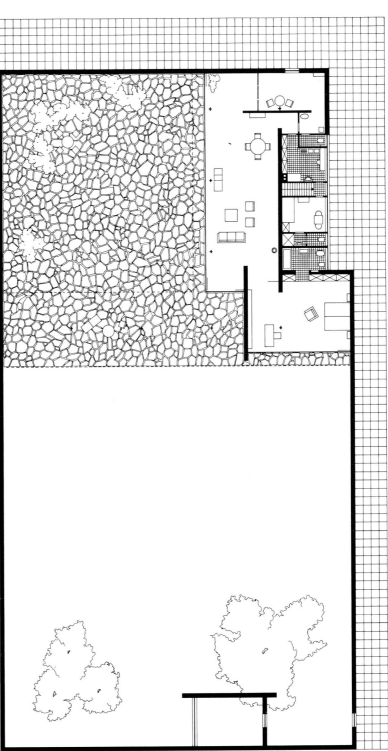

Atriumhaus, Projekt am Bauhaus
Dessau.

Atrium house project at the Bauhaus
Dessau.

Temporäres Wohnhaus auf der Berliner
Bauausstellung,
Mies van der Rohe, 1931

Ein regelmässiges Konstruktionssystem
über 8 Felder von 5 x 6 m mit allseitiger
Dachüberkragung von 3 m. Ein Hof als
intimer Terrassenraum umschliesst die
Schlaf- und Arbeitsbereiche, an deren
Ende ein spiegelndes Wasserbecken
das umgebende Patio abschliesst. Die
Skizzen Mies', die wechselnde Einsich-
ten vom gleichen Standort aus vermit-
teln, galten der Auseinandersetzung
zwischen Innen- und Aussenraum,
einem von Mauern eingeschlossenen
Wohnhof. In seinem Konstruktionsge-
füge sind Aussenwände ohne Tragfunk-
tionen. Es ging ihm um das Wechsel-
spiel von geschlossenen Raumpartien
und offenen Gartenbildern.

Temporary house at the Berlin building
exhibition,
Mies van der Rohe, 1931

The construction system is regular with
8 fields of 5 x 6 m and a roof canti-
levered for 3 m on all sides. A court in
the form of an intimate terrace sur-
rounds the bedroom and working areas
and terminates in a pool of reflecting
water. Mies's sketches, which show
changing views from the same stand-
point, bring out the contrasts between
indoors and outdoors and emphasize
the character of a courtyard surrounded by walls. The external walls
have no load-bearing function in his
design. Here the interplay of enclosed
spaces and open garden vistas is the
essential.

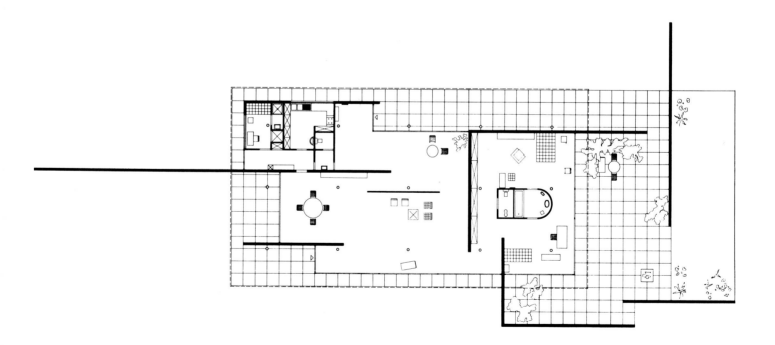

Haus auf der Berliner Bauausstellung
mit offenen Hofräumen, 1931,
Massstab 1:300.

House with open courts at the Berlin
building exhibition, 1931, scale 1:300.

Hofhausskizzen, Mies van der Rohe,
Berlin, 1931–1938

Die Hofhausidee war Mies' Alternative
in den dreissiger Jahren an Stelle frei-
stehender Einfamilienhäuser. Mit der
Idee des Atrium-Hauses wurden durch
die Gegenüberstellung von durchsichti-
gen und undurchsichtigen mobilen
Wänden neue Raumgestaltungsfor-
men entwickelt. Die Dachplatte ruht auf
den umschliessenden Hofmauern.

Courtyard house sketches,
Mies van der Rohe, Berlin 1931–38

In the thirties the courtyard house idea
was Mies's alternative to detached
single houses. The idea of the atrium
house was embodied in a new form by
the contrast created by opaque and
transparent screens round spaces. The
roof rests on the enclosing courtyard
walls.

Projekt für ein Haus mit drei Höfen,
1934, Massstab 1:300.

Project for a house with three courts,
1934, scale 1:300.

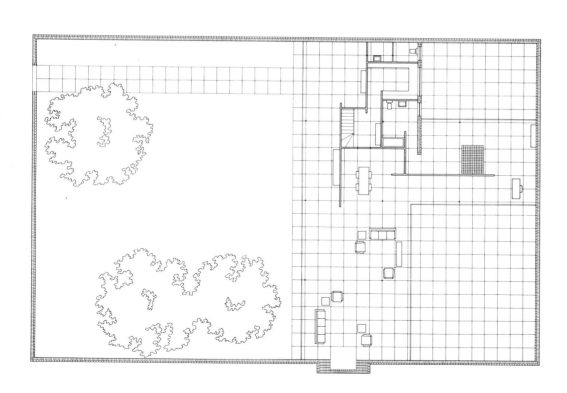

Füllfederskizze: Blick in einen Hof,
1934.

Fountain-pen sketch with view looking
into a court, 1934.

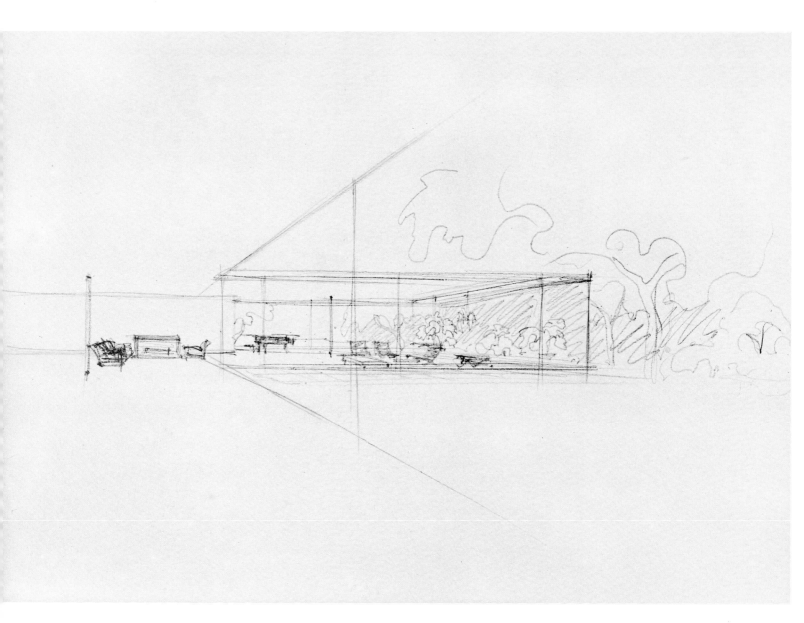

Skizzen für das Gericke-Haus am Wannsee, 1930.

Sketches for the Gericke House on the
Wannsee, 1930.

Skizzen für das Hubbe-Haus,
Mies van der Rohe, 1935

Haus Hubbe auf einer Insel in der Elbe
ist in zwei Konstruktionssysteme aufge-
teilt: der Stützenraster als Öffnung des
Raumes und die tragende Wand als
Raumabschluss charakterisieren das
Bauwerk. Durch die Öffnungen der Hofmauern sieht man in die weite Fluss-
landschaft.

Sketches for the Hubbe House,
Mies van der Rohe, 1935

The Hubbe House on an island in the
Elbe is divided into two structural sys-
tems. The grid pattern of supports
creating space and the load-bearing
walls forming the enclosure are the main
characteristics of the structure. A pavil-
ion-like building between two partially
enclosed courtyards affords a view of a
broad riverscape on the far side of the
courtyard walls.

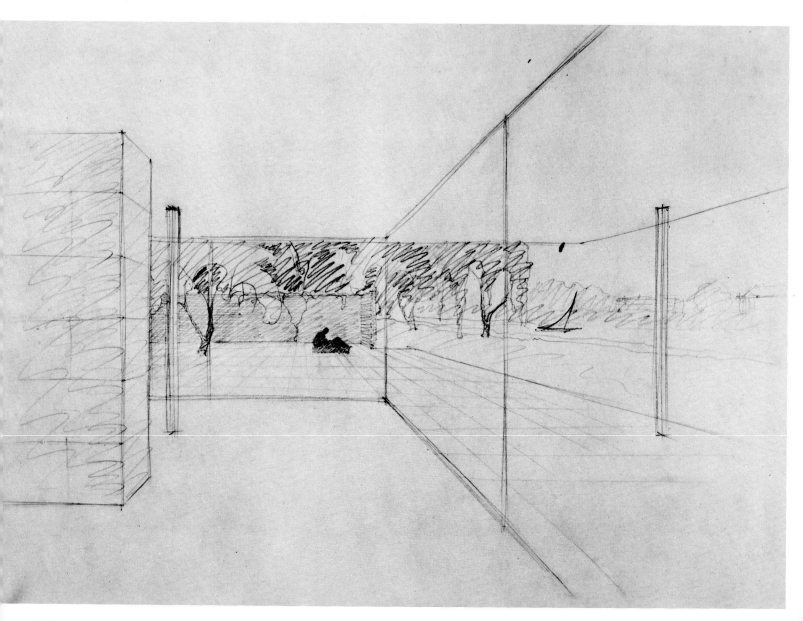

Skizze für das Hubbe-Haus in Magdeburg, 1935.

Sketch for the Hubbe House in Magdeburg, 1935.

Der Hof wird von einer Ziegelwand umschlossen.

The court is enclosed by a brick wall.

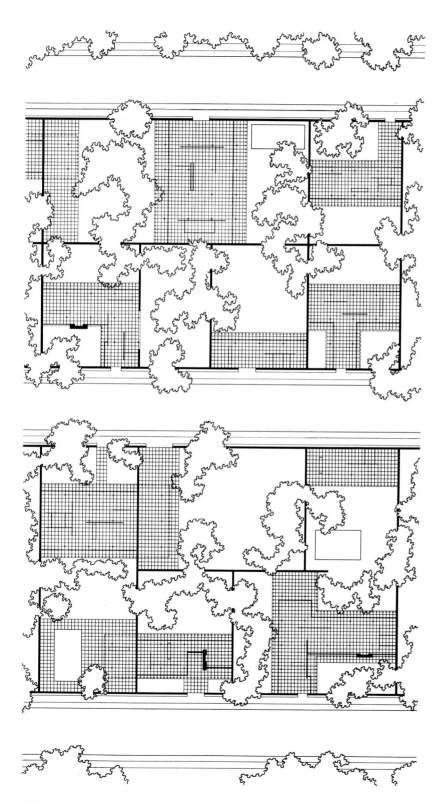

Teilplan einer Siedlung mit typischen Hofhäusern.

Detail of development plan with typical courtyard houses.

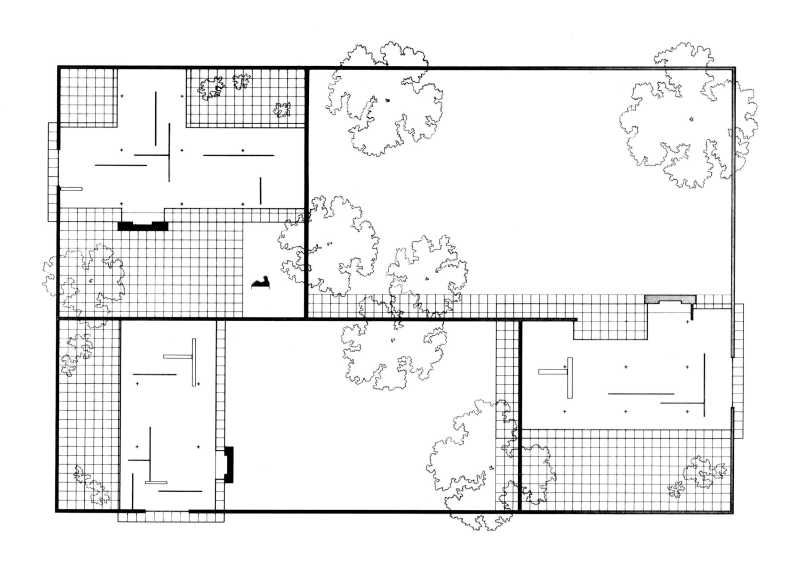

Gruppe von Hofhäusern, Massstab
1:400.

Group of courtyard houses, scale
1:400.

Studentenarbeit über Hofhäuser am IIT
(Illinois Institute of Technology),
Chicago.

Students' studies with courtyard houses
at IIT (Illinois Institute of Technology),
Chicago.

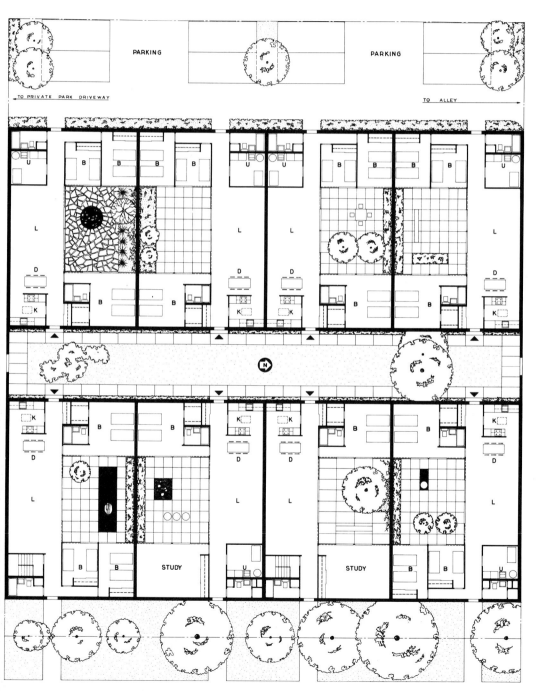

Atrium-Haustyp, Madison Park, Chicago,
Y.C. Wong, 1961

Acht Atrien als kompakte Wohnform in
einem innerstädtischen Wohngebiet,
mit überschaubar abgegrenztem
Wohnbereich ‹My home is my castle›.
Wohn- und Schlafräume orientieren sich
auf den Gartenhof und werden somit
optisch erweitert.

Atrium house type, Madison Park,
Chicago, Y.C. Wong, 1961

Eight atriums as a compact form of
housing in a downtown residential area
with a clear overview of the defined living space. 'My home is my castle'. The
living rooms and bedrooms are oriented
on the garden court and thus receive an
additional visual dimension.

170–177
Atriumhäuser in Chicago, Y.C. Wong.

Atrium houses in Chicago, Y.C. Wong.

170–175
Atriumhäuser, Madison Park, Chicago,
1961.

Atrium houses, Madison Park, Chicago,
1961.

170
Grundriss, Massstab 1:300.

Plan, scale 1:300.

171
Allee mit Eingängen zu den Häusern.

Avenue with entrances to the houses.

Der Hofgarten verbindet Innen und
Aussen.

The courtyard garden links indoors and
outdoors.

172

174–175
Die Privatsphäre wird durch den Hofraum geschaffen.

The courtyard creates an area of privacy.

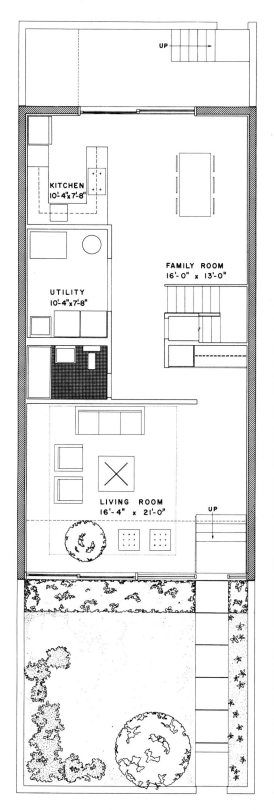
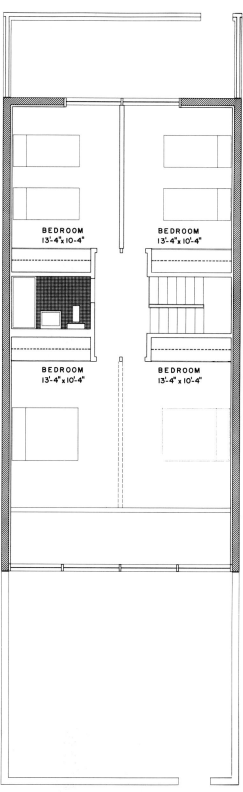

Reihenhauszeile mit Atrien, Hyde Park, Chicago, Y.C. Wong 1967

Reihenhauszeile als städtisches Hofhaus, ein zweigeschossiger Wohnbereich ist mit dem Gartenhof verbunden. Die Abstimmung des garden + townhouse nach aussen unter Einbeziehung des Gartenhofes ist in der Tradition der Chicago School realisiert.

Row houses with atriums, Hyde Park, Chicago, Y.C. Wong, 1967

Row houses as urban courtyard houses. A two-storey living area is linked with the garden court. The garden town house, matched to its environment outside and incorporating the garden court inside, is in the tradition of the Chicago School.

Reihenhäuser mit Atrien, 1967.

Row houses with atriums, 1967.

Sanierungsvorschlag mit Hofhäusern in Chicago, David Haid, 1967

Projected redevelopment with courtyard houses in Chicago, David Haid, 1967

Vorschlag einer typischen Sanierung eines Stadtviertels in Chicago mit Eigentumswohnungen in Atriumform mit grösseren Grünflächen, wo jede Familie ihr eigenes Haus mit Freiraum besitzt. Hohe Dichte soll mit einem Maximum an privater Sphäre vereint werden.

A typical redevelopment of an urban district in Chicago with condominium flats in atrium form and major verdant areas where each family has its own house with an open court. High density is combined with the maximum of privacy.

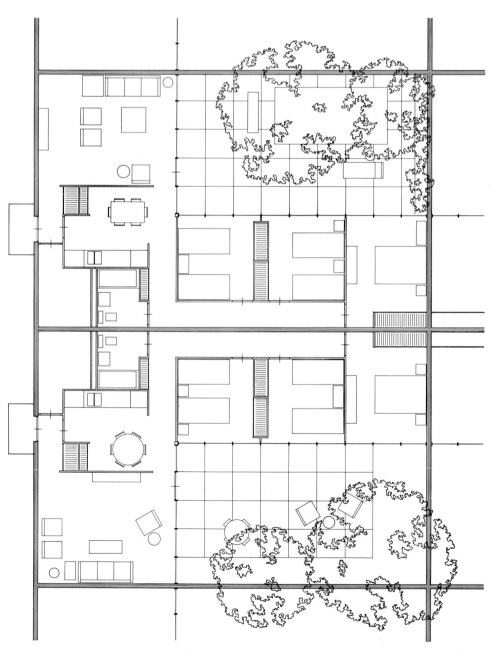

178–179
Hofhaussiedlung in Chicago, David Haid, 1967.

Courtyard house development in Chicago, David Haid, 1967.

178
Typischer Grundriss

Typical plan

Primarschule in Locarno-Saleggi, Livio
Vacchini, 1972–1979

Die Schultrakte, eingeschossige
Gebäude mit Innenhöfen, übernehmen
jeweils die Hauptrichtung der bestehenden angrenzenden Parzellierung.
Dieses Bauwerk mit den Hofanlagen
übernimmt damit mehr den Charakter
einer informell artikulierten Schule.
Durch die räumliche Staffelung wird der
Hof zum meditativen, befreienden Erleb-
nis.

Primary school in Locarno-Saleggi,
Livio Vacchini, 1972–79

The classroom blocks as single-storey
buildings with inner courts follow the
main alignment of the adjacent lots.
The layout with the courtyards thus
assumes the character of an informally
organized school. Because of the
staggered pattern, the courtyard is a
place conducive to meditation.

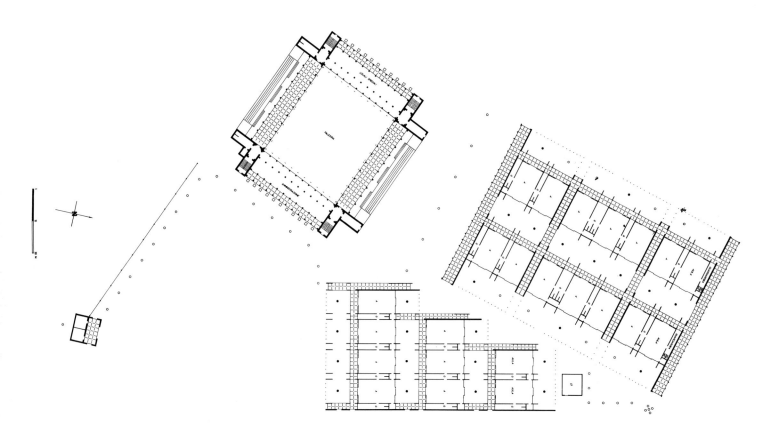

180–183
Höfe in Schulkomplexen, Livio Vacchini.

Courtyards in school complexes, Livio
Vacchini.

180–181
Scuole elementari, Locarno.

Schulanlage in Losone, Livio Vacchini,
Locarno, 1973–1975

School at Losone, Livio Vacchini,
Locarno, 1973–75

Die Schulanlage für die etwa 1000
Schüler der Scuola media unica ist in
vier Klassentrakte um einen Innenhof
aufgelöst, die zusammen eine architektonische Einheit bilden. Dieses System –
vier in Stahl konstruierte Gebäude in L-
Form – definiert den quadratischen
Hof.

A school for about 1000 pupils of the
scuola media unica, divided into four
classroom blocks arranged round an
inner courtyard and forming an architectural unit. This system consists of
four L-shaped buildings constructed in
steel which define a square courtyard.

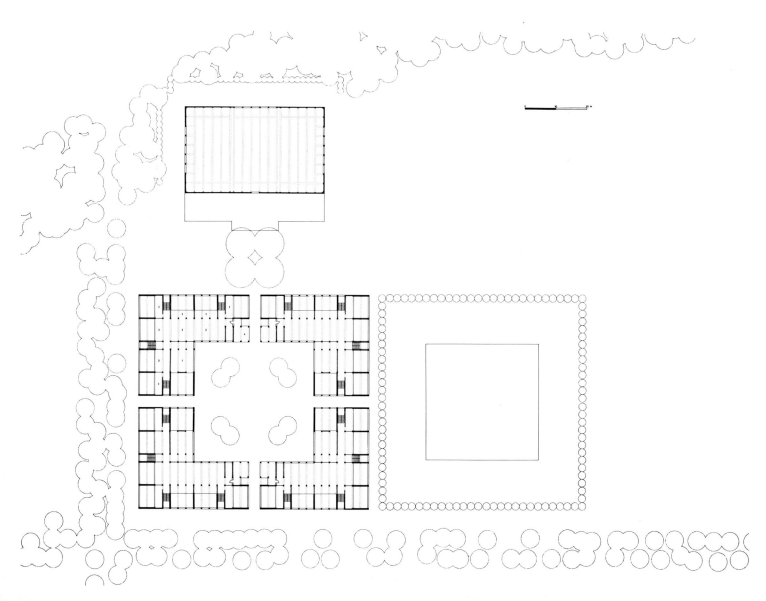

Semesterarbeit WS 1981/82, Hochschule für Angewandte Kunst, Wien, Meisterklasse für Innenarchitektur (Gastprofessor Werner Blaser).

Recherchen vom römischen Atrium bis zu den heutigen Hofhäusern. Entwicklung und Möblierung eines Hofhauses auf minimaler Parzelle nach Grundlagen des IIT, Chicago. Hofhaustypus L-förmig über zwei Stockwerke mit quadratischem Hof, wie eingeschossiges Hofhaus auf langgezogener Parzelle (Typ Reihenhaus).

Term work WS 1981/82, College of Applied Arts, Vienna. Master class for interior design (visiting professor, Werner Blaser).

Research from the Roman atrium to modern courtyard houses. Development and furnishing of a courtyard house on a minimal plot based on data from the Illinois Institute of Technology, Chicago. L-shaped type of courtyard house of two storeys with a square court, as well as a single-storey courtyard house on an elongated lot (row house type).

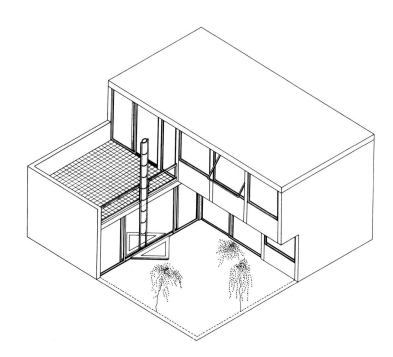

184–191
Semesterarbeit an der Hochschule für Angewandte Kunst, Wien.

Semester study at the College of Applied Arts, Vienna.

184–187
Zweistöckiges Hofhaus mit viereckigem Grundriss, Massstab 1:200.

Two-storey courtyard house on a square plan, scale 1:200.

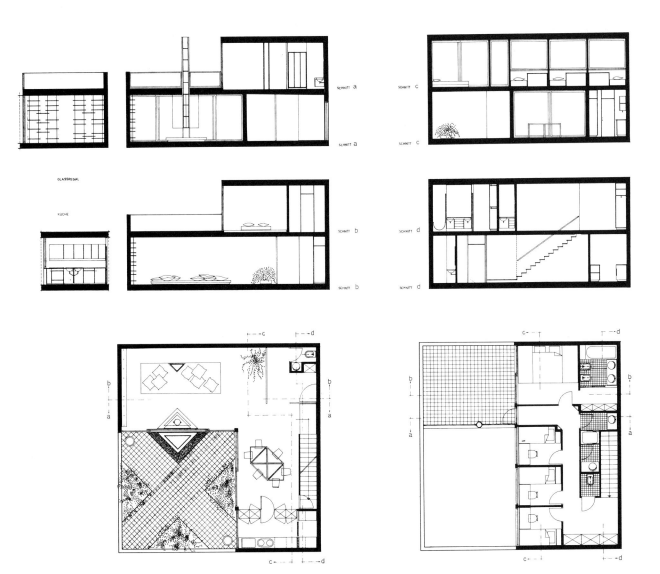

GLASSREGAL

KUCHE

SCHNITT a

SCHNITT a

SCHNITT b

SCHNITT b

SCHNITT c

SCHNITT c

SCHNITT d

SCHNITT d

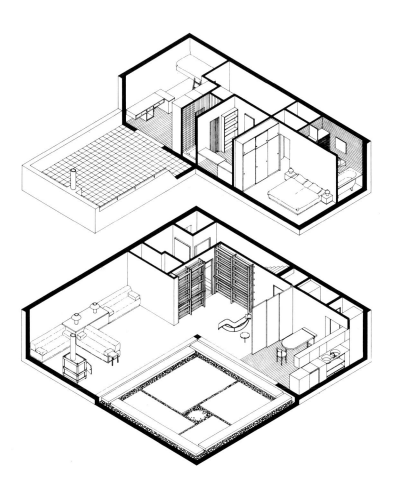

Variation mit viereckigem Grundriss,
Massstab 1:200.

Variation with square plan, scale 1:200.

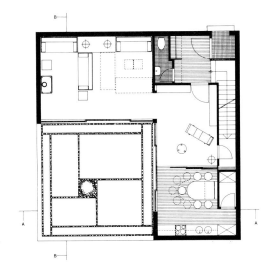

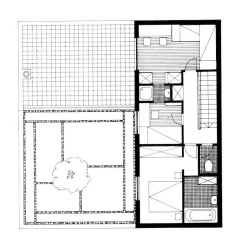

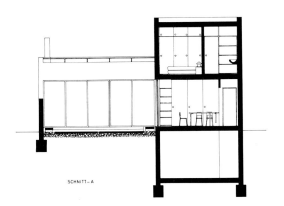

SCHNITT–A

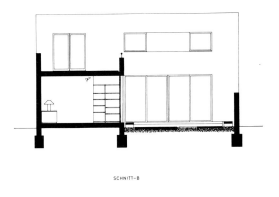

SCHNITT–B

187

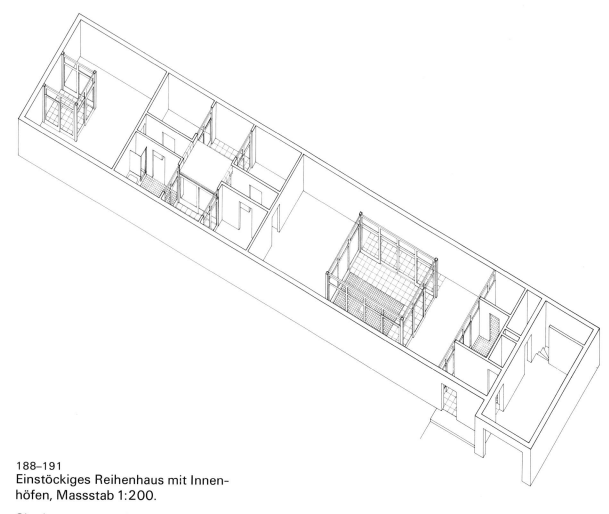

188–191
Einstöckiges Reihenhaus mit Innenhöfen, Massstab 1:200.

Single-storey row house with inner
courts, scale 1:200.

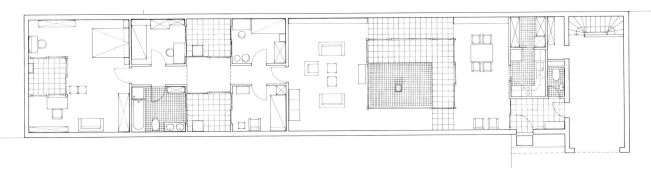

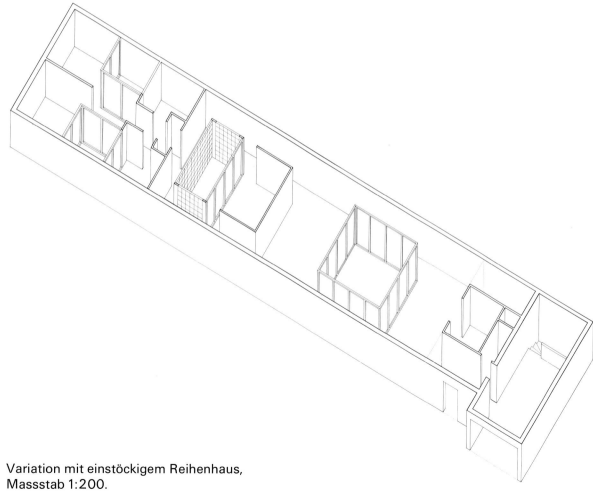

Variation mit einstöckigem Reihenhaus,
Massstab 1:200.

Variation with single-storey row house,
scale 1:200.

190

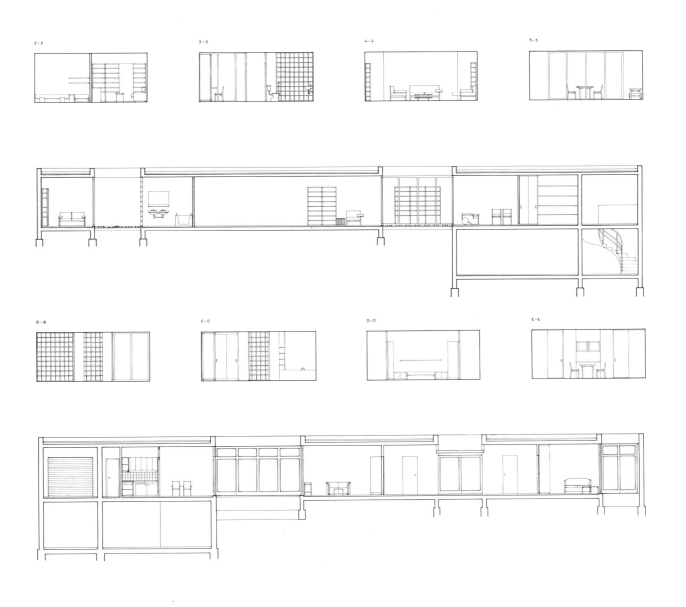

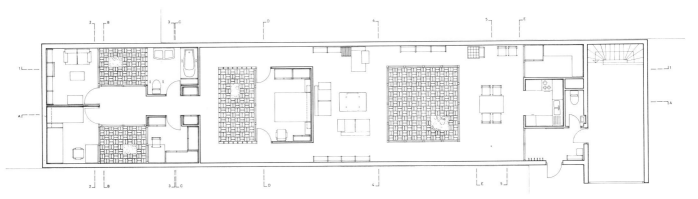

Gruppe von Hofhäusern aus einem Baukastensystem von Werner Blaser, Projekt 1975

Siedlungen von Hofhaustypen führen zu städtebaulichen Anordnungen intimer, abgeschlossener Wohnbezirke – zu eigentlichen Klausuren. Das rechteckige Grundstück von etwa 720 m² wird durch umlaufende Wandeinheiten von 1,20 m Breite und 2,40 m Höhe von der Umwelt abgeschirmt. Ein Teil des Hofes wird von einer Dachplatte überdeckt, unter der sich die Wohnräume befinden. Die Grundkonzeption vom Wohnen in der Parklandschaft zeigt eine Koordination von Innen und Aussen, d.h. von Raum und Garten. Das industriell hergestellte Baukastensystem und die Standardisierung der Wohnform – daher Ökonomie und Anpassung – ergeben eine wachsende Wohnung je nach individuellem Bedürfnis. Das erweiterbare Stahlskelett im Achsmass von 3,60/3,60 m und die veränderbaren Ausbauelemente von Fassade, Boden, Decke und Wand sind im Rastermodul von 1,20 m festgelegt.

Group of courtyard houses on the unit construction principle by Werner Blaser, project 1975

Projects with the courtyard type of house yield urban patterns of intimate, enclosed living areas – almost like monastic cells. The rectangular plot of about 720 m² is shut off from its surroundings by enclosing wall units 1.20 m wide and 2.40 m high. Part of the court is covered by a roofing slab under which the living rooms are set out. The basic concept underlying living in a parkland involves coordination of indoors and outdoors, that is, room and garden. The unit construction system is industrially produced and the layout is standardized, thus making for economy and adaptation. The unit can be increased in size to meet requirements. The steel skeleton, which can be extended, has axial dimensions of 3.60/3.60. The facade, floor, ceiling and wall elements can be altered. A grid module of 1.20 m is used.

192–195
Hofhausprojekte, Werner Blaser.

Courtyard house projects, Werner Blaser.

193
Hofhausidee aus einem Baukasten.

Courtyard house on unit construction principle.

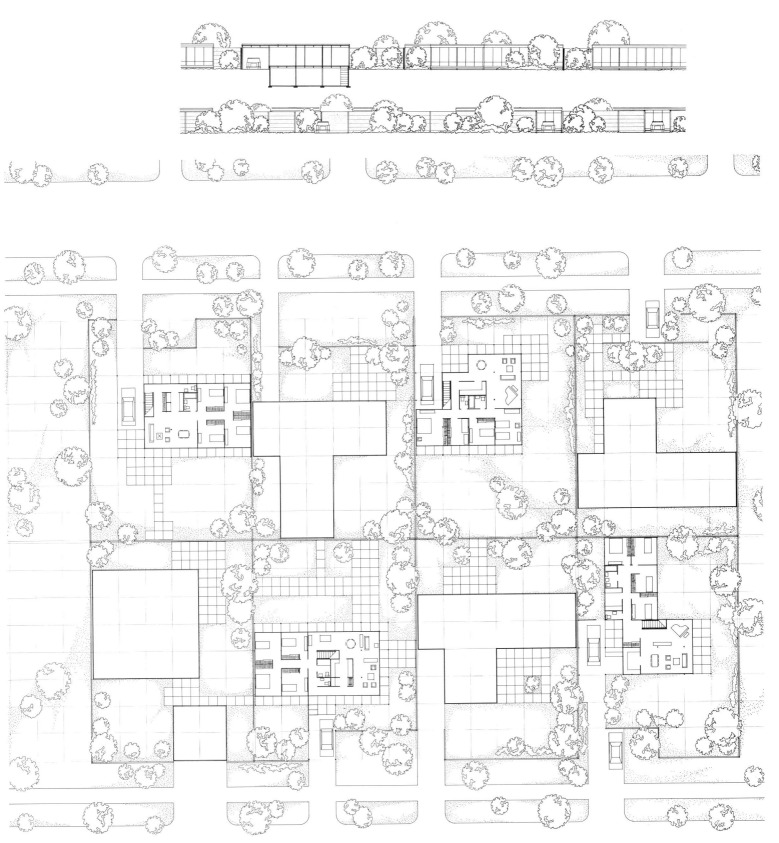

193

Hofhausprojekt, 1975.

Courtyard house project, 1975.

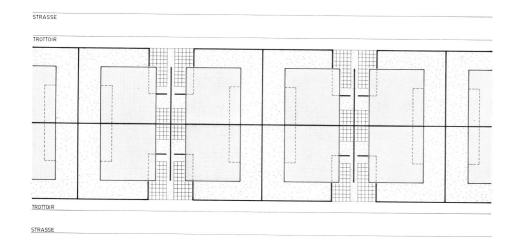

STRASSE

TROTTOIR

TROTTOIR

STRASSE

194
Situation Gruppe von Hofhäusern,
Massstab 1:500.

General plan of group of courtyard
houses, scale 1:500.

195
Patios in allen vier Himmelsrichtungen,
Massstab 1:200.

Patios to all four points of the compass,
scale 1:200.

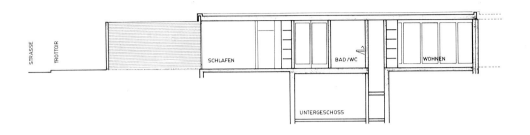

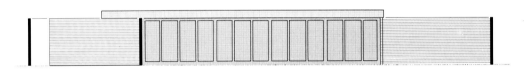

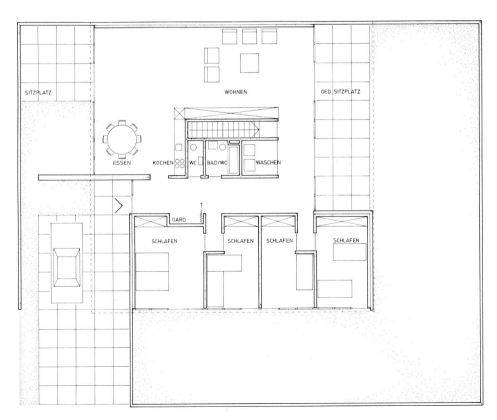

Wander Bertoni – Ausstellungsbau und Wohnung von Johannes Spalt, Wien 1975–1976

Das Haus Wander Bertoni, in Grinzing gelegen, ist ein Zu- und Umbau und muss verschiedene Aufgaben erfüllen. Es ist um einen Hof in Verbindung zu dem bestehenden Gebäude angeordnet und dient vor allem als Ausstellungsbau für Plastiken. Der mittlere, höhere Teil hat eine schürzenartige Wand zum Hof hin und damit eine beabsichtigte Beziehung zur Grünfläche. Das Dach ist an den Rändern halbrund heruntergezogen und wirkt dadurch raumschliessend. Die Konstruktion dieses aus Holz gebauten Hauses hat – mit spantenartigen Hölzern und einer Beplankung – Ähnlichkeit mit einem umgekehrten Schiffsrumpf.

Wander Bertoni – exhibition building and flat by Johannes Spalt, Vienna, 1975–1976

The Wander Bertoni House, located in Grinzing, is both an extension and a conversion and has a number of functions to fulfil. It is primarily an exhibition building for sculptures and is arranged round a courtyard and connected with the existing building. The middle portion, which is higher, has an apron-like wall facing the yard and is thus deliberately related to the verdant area. The edges of the roof are extended downward in a half-round shape as if to close

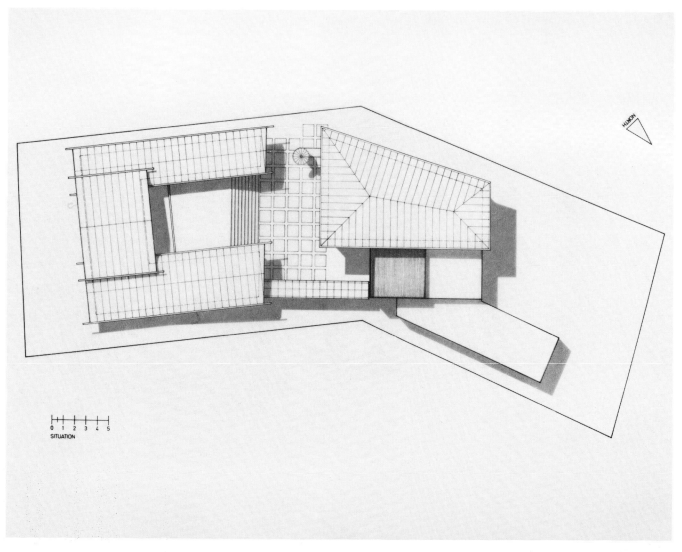

0 1 2 3 4 5
SITUATION

NORTH

off space. In structure this timber-built
house resembles an upturned boat. It
has rib-like timbers and is planked.

Ausstellungsbau für den Bildhauer
Wander Bertoni von Johannes Spalt,
Wien, 1976.

Exhibition building for the sculptor
Wander Bertoni, by Johannes Spalt,
Vienna, 1976.

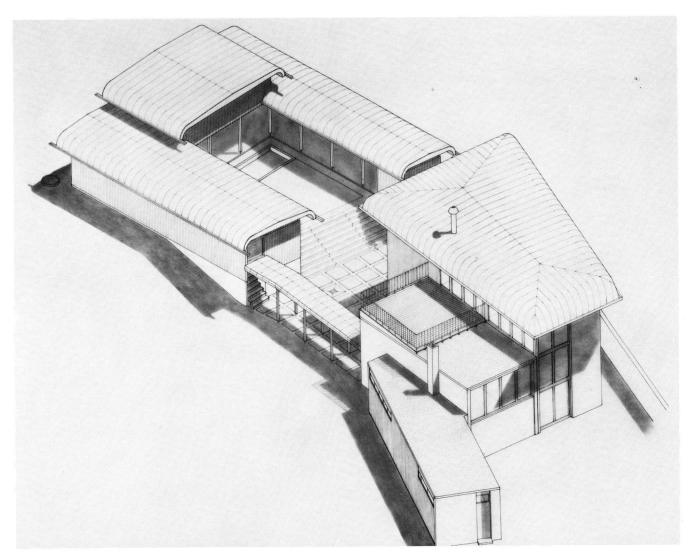

Schweizerischer Bankverein, Wiederaufbau Sitzgebäude Basel, Suter + Suter Generalplaner, 1984.

Architektur in der Dialektik mit der Natur. Der Lichthof mit einem Ahornbaum bringt Licht und Vegetation bis ins Innere des Gebäudes. Die Lichtquelle wurde zu einem wünschenswerten städtebaulichen Verknüpfungsprinzip.

Swiss Bank Corporation, reconstruction of headquarters office, Basle, Suter + Suter, general planners, 1984.

Architecture in dialogue with nature. The patio with a maple tree brings light and greenery into the centre of the building. The light well has acquired a legitimate position in urban development as an indoor-outdoor link.

198–203
Lichthof des Schweizerischen Bankvereins in Basel, 1984.

Light well, Swiss Bank Corporation in Basle, 1984.

199
Ein ‹Atrium› im Bankgebäude: Innenraum ist Aussenraum im Innenraum. Die Jahreszeit dringt ins Innere der Schalterhalle.

An 'atrium' in the bank building: the interior is the exterior brought into the interior. The seasons come into the banking hall.

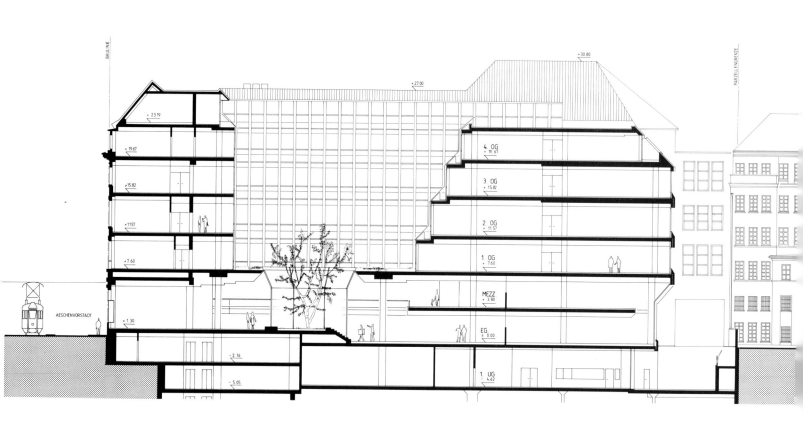

200
Schnitt, Massstab 1:400.

Section, scale 1:400.

201
Grundriss im 3. Obergeschoss, Massstab 1:400.

Plan on 3rd floor, scale 1:400.

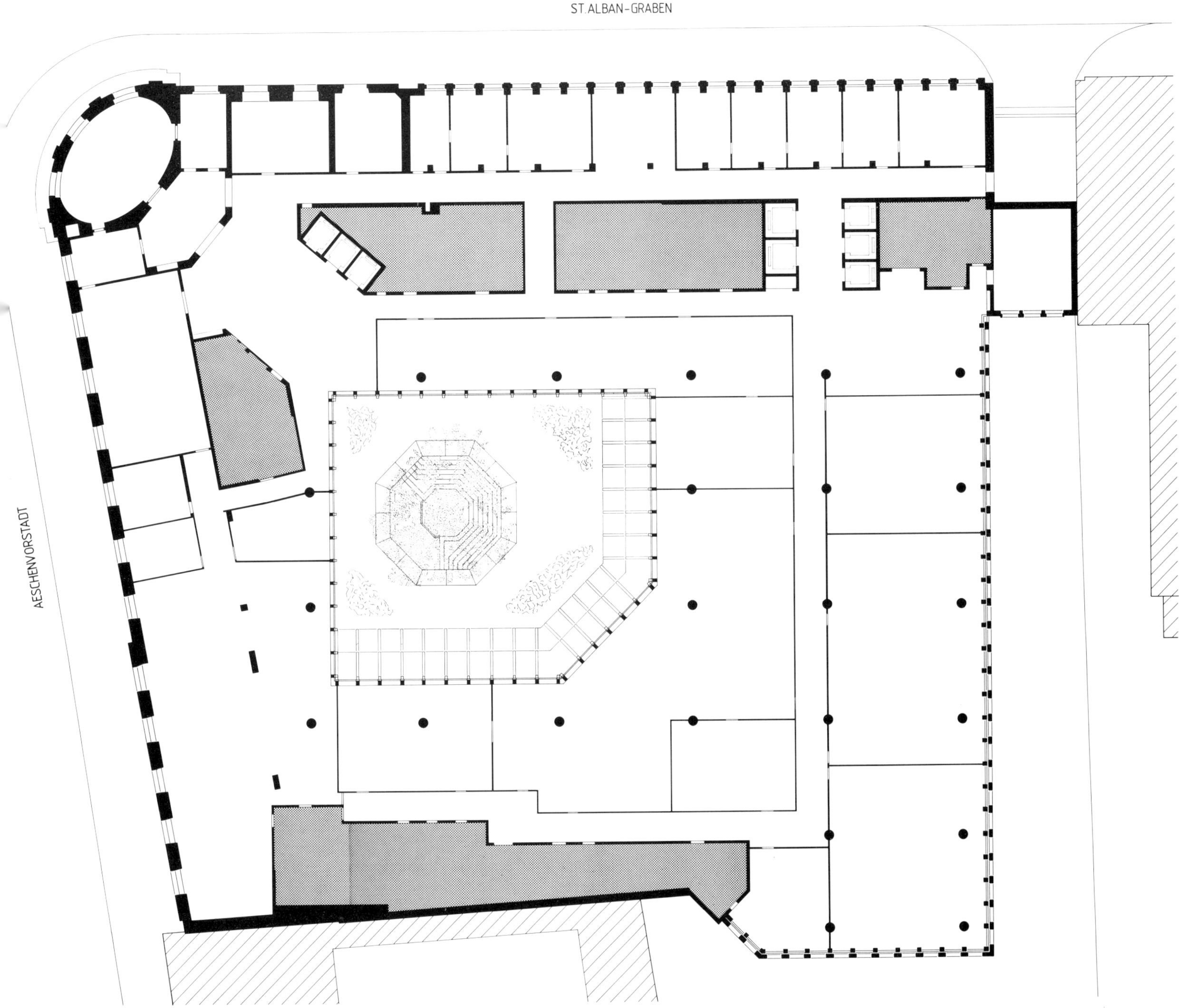

ST.ALBAN-GRABEN

AESCHENVORSTADT

202–203
Der Ahorn im Frühling und im Winter.

The maple in spring and winter.

Nachwort

Das Hofhaus ist immer noch eine der ursprünglichsten Wohnformen im Fernen Osten, im Islam und im Abendland. Je nach Art der Gestaltung unterscheidet man den Arkaden- oder Laubenhof, den Säulen- oder Peristylhof, den Baum- oder Gartenhof. Der Freiraum des Hofes ist ringsum oder an mehreren Seiten von Gebäuden oder Mauern umschlossen. In der spanischen und ibero-amerikanischen Baukunst nennen wir den offenen Innenhof ‹Patio›. Den Grundtyp des Lichthofes bei uns finden wir im ‹Atrium› verwirklicht und im Lexikon der Weltarchitektur wie folgt beschrieben:
‹Atrium (lateinisch), der innere Wohnhof des römischen Privathauses, an den sich Kammern und Wohngemächer anschlossen. Ursprünglich der Wohnraum mit dem Herdfeuer (daher auch der Raum für den Ahnenkult), entwickelt es sich zum säulenumstandenen Repräsentationsraum. In der frühchristlichen und maurischen Baukunst ein der Kirche vorgelagerter, meist viereckiger, von einer Säulenhalle umschlossener Hof, auch Paradies genannt, mit einem Brunnen (Kanthavos) für die rituellen Handlungen›.
Die vorliegende Arbeit ist das Ergebnis der Zusammenarbeit hauptsächlich mit meinem Kollegen und Freund Johannes Spalt, Professor an der Hochschule für Angewandte Kunst in Wien. In seiner Meisterklasse für Innenarchitektur und Industrieentwurf machte ich 1981/82 eine Semesterarbeit über das Hofhaus. Die Planzeichnungen im Massstab 1:200 der klassischen Hofhäuser, sowie die Darstellung und Möblierung heutiger Lösungen wurden von den Studenten der Meisterklasse bearbeitet. Diese Zeichnungen wurden von folgenden Studenten ausgeführt: Seite 35 Cornelia Senn, Seiten 69 und 117 Martin Stampfer, Seite 93 Walter Lauterer, Seite 111 Klara Grabner, Seiten 184, 185 Gorgona Staut, Seiten 186, 187 Hans Diblik, Seiten 188, 189 Wolfgang Exner,

Seiten 190, 191 M. Lang und H. Hutterer. Ihnen gehört mein aufrichtiger Dank. Um aber den Leser über das Hofhaus gründlich zu informieren, hatte Johannes Spalt die Geschichte des Hofhauses geschrieben und mit eigenen Skizzen illustriert. Mein Dank gilt ihm dafür, dass er diesen Beitrag zu einem eigentlichen Kompendium gemacht hat.

Das Atriumbuch ist das vierte Buch aus der Buchserie: ‹Der Fels ist mein Haus›, ‹Filigran Architektur› und ‹Holz Haus›. Es ist eine Genugtuung, mit einem Verlag, der schon Bücher über die Pionierarchitektur meines früheren Lehrers Paul Artaria herausbrachte, zu arbeiten. Robert Wepf sei dafür aufrichtig gedankt. Der Text wurde von Beate Berczelly sprachlich überarbeitet und von D.Q. Stephenson ins Englische übersetzt.
Die Beispiele der Hofhäuser bieten weiten Kreisen der heutigen Generation eine vorzügliche Möglichkeit, sich zu orientieren und in der Übernahme bestimmter Tendenzen unserer Zeit eigene Standpunkte zu finden. Dabei ist erstaunlich, wie viele Möglichkeiten und Veränderungen von heutigen Hofhausformen einer geistigen Bemühung wert sein können.

Postscript

The courtyard house continues to be one of the most original forms of dwelling in the Far East, Islam and the West. Depending on design, we can distinguish the arcaded courtyard, the pillared courtyard or peristyle, and the tree or garden courtyard. The courtyard is enclosed on all or several sides by buildings or walls. In Spanish and Hispano-American architecture the open inner court is called the 'patio'. The basic type of open court takes the form of an atrium with us and is defined in the Lexicon of World Architecture as follows: 'Atrium, the (Lat.) inner court of the Roman private house with adjoining chambers and living rooms. Originally the living room with the fire-hearth (and therefore also the room for ancestor worship), it developed into a room used for social purposes and was surrounded by pillars. In Early Christian and Moorish architecture, a courtyard in front of the church, usually square in shape and enclosed by a colonnade (also known as a paradise), with a fountain (kanthavos) for ritual consecrations.' The present work is the result of a joint effort in which a leading role was taken by my colleague and friend Johannes Spalt, professor at the College of Applied Arts in Vienna. In his master class for interior and industrial design in 1981/82 I did a term work on the courtyard house. A drawing of the plan of classical courtyard houses on a scale of 1:200 as well as the presentation and furnishing of modern designs of such houses constituted the task given to the students of the master class. These drawings were done by the following students: p. 35 Cornelia Senn, pp. 37, 69 and 117 Martin Stampfer, p. 93 Walter Lauterer, p. 111 Klara Grabner, pp. 184–185 Gorgona Staut, pp. 186–187 Hans Diblik, pp. 188–189 Wolfgang Exner, pp. 190–191 M. Lang and H. Hutterer. To them I am deeply indebted. To provide the reader with a full account of the courtyard house, Johannes Spalt has written its history illustrated with his own sketches. I am grateful to him for making this work into a veritable compendium.

The atrium house is the fourth book in the series: 'The Rock is my Home', 'Filigree Architecture' and 'Wood Houses'. It is a pleasure for me to work with a publisher who has already brought out studies of the pioneer architecture of my former teacher Paul Artaria. My sincere thanks go to Robert Wepf. The text was translated into English by D.Q. Stephenson.

The examples of the courtyard houses afford a wide circle of readers, particularly the younger generation, an excellent opportunity to take stock and to find their bearings amidst certain contemporary trends. It is astonishing to think how well it repays the intellectual effort involved to produce variations on the theme of the modern courtyard house and to explore its possibilities.

Bibliographie der benützten Literatur
Bibliography of literature consulted

Westliche Häuser und Höfe
Herbert Kürth, Baustilfibel, Volk und Wissen Volkseigener Verlag, Berlin DDR, 1984
Nikolaus Pevsner, Lexikon der Weltarchitektur, Prestel-Verlag, München, 1971
Hans Koepf, Bildwörterbuch der Architektur, Alfred Kröner Verlag, Stuttgart, 1974
Wend Fischer, Geborgenheit und Freiheit – Vom Bauen mit Glas, Scherpe Verlag, Krefeld, 1970

Islamisches Stadtwesen
Ulya Vogt-Göknil, Osmanische Türkei, Office du Livre, Fribourg, 1965
Marino Antequera, Die Alhambra und der Generalife, Ediciones Miguel Sanchez, Granada, 1982
Maurice Besset, Who was Le Corbusier, Editions Skira, Genève, 1968
Ernst Egli, Sinan, Verlag für Architektur, Zürich, 1954

Fernöstliche Hofhäuser
Robert A. Rorex, The Story of Lady Wenchi, The Metropolitan Museum of Art, New York, 1974
Vittorio Gregotti, Rassegna-Problemi di architettura dell' ambiente, Milano, 1979
Werner Blaser, Hofhaus in China, Birkhäuser Verlag, Basel, 1979
Chen Cong-zhou, The Gardens of Yangzhou, Shanghai, 1980
Lee Chien-Lang, A Survey of Kinmen Traditional Architecture, Taipei, 1978
Thomas Thilo, Klassische Chinesische Baukunst, Edition Tusch, Wien, 1977
Eduardo Sacriste, Huellas de Edificios, Editorial Universitaria de Buenos Aires, 1962
Tetsuro Yoshida, Der Japanische Garten, Verlag Ernst Wasmuth, Tübingen, 1957
Heinrich Engel, The Japanese House, Charles E. Tuttle, Publisher, Tokyo, 1964

Rurale Hofhaustypen
Häuser und Höfe auf Skansen, Stockholm, 1979
Marie-Noël Denis, Alsace, Berger-Levrault, éditeur, Paris, 1978
Roland Rainer, Anonymes Bauen: Nordburgenland, Verlag Galerie Welz, Salzburg, 1961
Werner Blaser, Strukturale Architektur aus Osteuropa, Zbinden Verlag, Basel, 1975

Klosterhof mit Kreuzgang
Pierre Charpentrat, Barock, Office du Livre, Fribourg, 1964
Werner Blaser, Objektive Architektur, Scherpe Verlag, Krefeld, 1970

Patios der Kolonial-Architektur
Beatrice Trueblood, Vivienda Campesina en México, 1978

Hofhäuser des 20. Jahrhunderts
Vittorio Magnago Lampugnani, Lexikon der Architektur des 20. Jhs., Verlag Gerd Hatje, Stuttgart, 1983
Heinrich Tessenow, Hausbau und dergleichen, Woldemar Klein Verlag, Baden-Baden, 1953
Oswald W. Grube, 100 Jahre Architektur in Chicago, Die Neue Sammlung, München, 1973
James Speyer, Mies van der Rohe, The Art Institute of Chicago, 1968
Werner Blaser, Mies van der Rohe, Die Kunst der Struktur, Verlag für Architektur, Zürich, 1965
Werner Blaser, Mies van der Rohe, Continuing the Chicago School of Architecture, Birkhäuser Verlag, Basel, 1981
Werner Blaser, Architecture 70/80 in Switzerland, Birkhäuser Verlag, Basel, 1982
Werner Blaser, Architektur im Möbel, Waser Verlag, Zürich, 1985

Weitere Bücher dieser Reihe:

Werner Blaser hat seine Beobachtungen und visuellen Erfahrungen in unzähligen Fotografien fixiert. Eine Auswahl vom Besten zeigt und kommentiert er in der vorliegenden Buchreihe über Architektur in Stein, Holz, Glas und Metall.

Other books in this series:

Werner Blaser has given his observations and visual experiences a permanent form in innumerable photographs. In the present series of books on architecture in stone, wood, glass and metal he presents a selection of the best of these pictures and adds his comments.

Der Fels ist mein Haus

Bauwerke in Stein

Das Material Stein und seine Verwendung werden in den elementarsten Grundlagen geschildert: Stein kommt auf Stein, es entsteht ein kompaktes Gebilde und wirkt wie ein Fels, der zum bergenden Heim wird. Materie, Konstruktion und Lebensform sind hier eins. Das reiche Fotomaterial zeigt Beispiele aus dem südlichen Alpengebiet (Tessin, Graubünden) und von der Aran-Insel Inisheer im Atlantik vor Irland.
224 Seiten mit 142 Fotos und 28 Planzeichnungen. Text dreisprachig: deutsch, französisch, englisch. Zürich 1976

The rock is my home

Structures in stone

Stone as a material and the uses man has made of it are shown from the earliest beginnings when one stone was simply laid on another. The structure grew, became rock-like in its compactness, and provided shelter for a home. Here material, construction and way of life become one. The numerous photographs show examples from the southern Alps (Grisons, Ticino) and from Inisheer, one of the Aran Islands in the Atlantic off Ireland.
224 pages with 142 photos and 28 plans.
Text in German, French and English. Zurich 1976.

Holz Haus

Rurale Bauform

Block- und Ständerbauten aus dem alpinen und voralpinen Raum der Schweiz, urtümliche Fachwerkbauten aus dem Elsass und von der Industrie beeinflusste Holzhäuser aus den Städten Südwestfinnlands bilden das Thema dieses Bandes. Der Autor zeigt uns die Vielfalt der Materie «Holz» als Konstruktionselement. Es geht Werner Blaser darum, die konstruktiven Probleme heimischer Bausubstanz kennenzulernen, zu durchdenken und mit neuen Impulsen zu versehen. Das Element Holz wird in seinen Möglichkeiten und Grenzen im Bauen – auch in der heutigen Zeit – gewürdigt.
224 Seiten mit 127 Fotos und 68 Zeichnungen. Text dreisprachig: deutsch, französisch, englisch. 2. erweiterte Aufl., gebunden. Basel, 1985.

Wood houses

Form in rural architecture

Primitive log and timber-framed structures in the Alpine and sub-Alpine parts of Switzerland, unsophisticated half-timbered buildings in Alsace, and wood houses in the towns of southwest Finland which were influenced by industry are the subject of this book. The author acquaints us more closely with the multifarious properties of the material 'wood'. Werner Blaser is concerned to investigate the structural problems of the native heritage of architecture, to think out its implications, and to make its virtues better known. He values wood as a building material at its true worth – both in the past and today – and assesses its potentialities as well as its limitations.
224 pages with 127 photos and 68 drawings.
Text in German, French and English. Basel 1980.

Filigran Architektur

Metall- und Glaskonstruktion

Dieses Werk zeigt mit bestechenden Bildern sensible Gusseisenarchitektur, Hallenbauten des Maschinenzeitalters und die Entwicklung der «Skin and Skeleton» Architektur seit dem letzten Jahrhundert bis in die neueste Zeit.
Es gliedert sich in zwei Teile: die europäische Architekturentwicklung einerseits und das amerikanische Bauen andererseits, insbesondere die Vorherrschaft der ersten und zweiten «Chicago School of Architecture». Also die traditionsreichen europäischen Tendenzen im Gegensatz zur Entwicklung in den Vereinigten Staaten, die frei von verpflichtendem Erbe verlief.
216 Seiten mit 106 Fotos und 89 Zeichnungen. Text dreisprachig: deutsch, französisch, englisch. Basel, 1980.

Filigree architecture

Metal and glass construction

This work is a fascinating account of sensitively designed cast-iron architecture, of hall structures of the Machine Age, and of the development of 'skin-and-skeleton' architecture from the last century down to the present day. It is divided into two parts: the development of European architecture on the one hand and American construction on the other, particularly the ascendancy of the first and second 'Chicago School of Architecture'. In other words, European tendencies with their commitment to tradition are contrasted with developments in the United States, where there is no inheritance to exert its influence.
216 pages with 106 photos and 89 drawings. Text in German, French and English. Basel 1980.

Werner Blaser gehört der unmittelbaren Nachfolgegeneration der Architekturpioniere unseres Jahrhunderts an. Als Schüler von Alvar Aalto und Mies van der Rohe hat er nicht nur die Kontinuität der Architekturentwicklung in ihrer Multimedialität bewahrt, sondern sie auch multimedial durchdacht und in einer konsequenten Dichte angewendet, wie sie nur wenige Persönlichkeiten seiner Generation nachweisen können. Werner Blaser hat vor über 25 Jahren seine Sicht, sein Prinzip der Architektur entwickelt und diese über die Fotografie, das Design, den Baukörper und Publikationen gleichbedeutend zum Ausdruck gebracht. Als einer der selten gewordenen, universalbegabten und -tätigen Architektentypen gibt er nicht vor, die Architektur nochmals erfinden zu müssen; ihm ist bewusst, dass unsere Antwort auf unsere Zeit nur in Reflexion auf die Vergangenheit formuliert werden kann.

Seine Beobachtungen und visuellen Erfahrungen hat Werner Blaser in unzähligen Fotos fixiert. Durch das Instrument der Kamera expliziert er, wie das Auge als Organ der Erkenntnis wirksam wird und wie im Abbild des Geschauten das Erkannte auch dem Beschauer sinnfällig vermittelt werden kann. Hans Hartmann über Werner Blaser.

Werner Blaser is one of the generation following immediately upon the architectural pioneers of our century. As a pupil of Alvar Aalto and Mies van der Rohe he has not only preserved the continuity of architectural development in its multimediality but has also thought out its multimedial implications and applied them with a strict conformity to rigid principles such as few personalities of his generation can rival. Over a period of 25 years Werner Blaser has developed his view, his principle, of architecture and expressed it with equal validity in photography, design, construction and publications. As one of that now rare type of architect who is universally gifted and active he does not claim that he has to reinvent architecture afresh; he is aware that our response to our own times can only be formulated by reflection on the past.

Werner Blaser has recorded his observations and visual experiences in countless photographs. Through the camera he shows how the eye can be the instrument of knowledge and how, by the perceived image, what has been newly discovered can be forcefully conveyed to the viewer. Hans Hartmann on Werner Blaser.